P9-EDD-201

Sterling Silver, Silverplate and Souvenir Spoons

with prices

10th Printing 2003

© August 1987

L-W Book Sales
Box 69
Gas City, IN 46933

Table of Contents

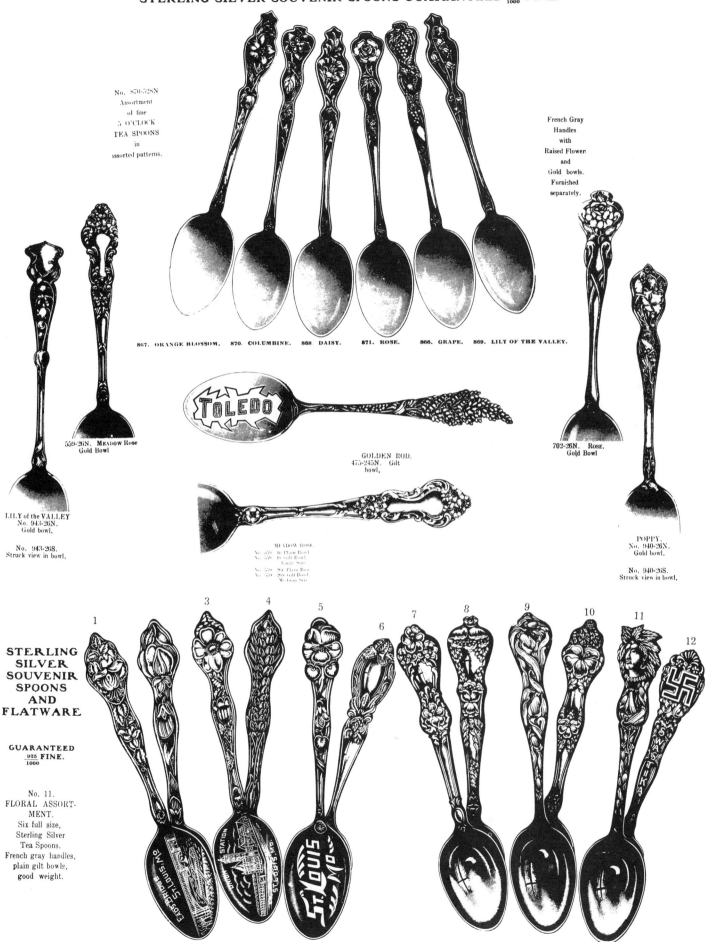

No. 870-52SN
Assortment
of fine
5 O'CLOCK
TEA SPOONS
in
assorted patterns.

French Gray
Handles
with
Raised Flowers
and
Gold bowls.
Furnished
separately.

559-26N. MEADOW ROSE
Gold Bowl

867. ORANGE BLOSSOM. 870. COLUMBINE. 868. DAISY. 871. ROSE. 866. GRAPE. 869. LILY OF THE VALLEY.

TOLEDO

GOLDEN ROD.
475-245N. Gilt
bowl,

702-26N. ROSE.
Gold Bowl.

LILY of the VALLEY
No. 943-26N.
Gold bowl,

No. 943-26S.
Struck view in bowl,

MEADOW ROSE

POPPY.
No. 940-26N.
Gold bowl.

No. 940-26S.
Struck view in bowl,

STERLING
SILVER
SOUVENIR
SPOONS
AND
FLATWARE

GUARANTEED
$\frac{925}{1000}$ FINE.

No. 11.
FLORAL ASSORT-
MENT.
Six full size,
Sterling Silver
Tea Spoons.
French gray handles,
plain gilt bowls,
good weight.

1

STERLING SILVER FLORAL SOUVENIR TEA SPOONS.
FRENCH GRAY HANDLES. GUARANTEED $\frac{925}{1000}$ FINE.

SUNFLOWER
No. 516 18 Gilt Bowl

61-528N. COLUMBINE.
Gold Bowl -

702-26N. ROSE.
Gold Bowl -

750-26N. POND LILY.
Gold Bowl -

765-26N. COLUMBINE.
Gold Bowl -

559-26N. MEADOW ROSE.
Gold Bowl -

TEDDY BEAR.
No. 816 26 Plain Bowl.
No. 816 28 Gilt Bowl.

SWASTIKA.
No. 84 28 Struck
Bow and Arrow in Bowl.
No. 84 Plain or Gilt

SEGO LILY.
No. 574 18 Gilt Bowl

No. 485-2B. Pineapple.
Plain bowl.
No. 485-2N. Pineapple.
Gilt bowl.

No. 548-2B. Cantelope.
Plain bowl.
No. 548-2N. Cantelope.
Gilt bowl.

No. 370-2B. Orange.
Plain bowl.
No. 370-2N Orange.
Gilt bowl.

FORGET-ME-NOT.
No. 443 18 Gilt Bowl

No. 288-2B. Poppy.
Plain bowl.
No. 288-2N. Poppy.
Gilt bowl.

AMERICAN INDIAN.
No. 409 24B Plain Bowl
No. 409 24N Gilt Bowl

45-26N. SWEET CLOVER.
Gold Bowl -

717-26N. DAISY.
Gold Bowl -

714-26N. PINE CONE
Gold Bowl -

723-26N. SAGO LILY
Gold Bowl!

BUCKING BRONCO.
435-48. Struck,

MINER.
409-245B. Plain

61-528N. COLUMBINE.
Gold Bowl

2

STERLING SILVER

BIRTHDAY SPOON.
For Any Month.
No. **5831**.   Raised figures, gold bowl, French gray handle.

STERLING SILVER

Easter Spoon.   Gold Plated, Enameled Cross.
No. **8204** .

Easter Spoon.   Gold Plated, Enameled Design in Bowl.
No. **8205** .

Easter Spoon.   Gold Lined Engraved Bowl, Bright Handle.
No. **8206** .

Souvenir Spoon.   French Grey Finished Handle, Gold Lined Bowl.
No. **8207** .

Orange Spoon.   French Grey Finished Handle, Gold Lined Bowl.
No. **8208** .

Orange Spoon.   Bright Finished Handle, Gold Lined Bowl.
No. **8209** .

Solid Sterling Silver Souvenir Spoons

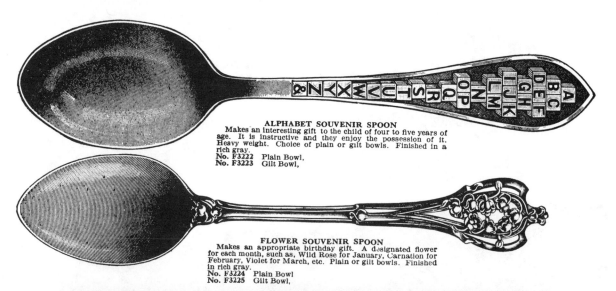

ALPHABET SOUVENIR SPOON

Makes an interesting gift to the child of four to five years of age. It is instructive and they enjoy the possession of it. Heavy weight. Choice of plain or gilt bowls. Finished in a rich gray.
No. F3222   Plain Bowl,
No. F3223   Gilt Bowl,

FLOWER SOUVENIR SPOON

Makes an appropriate birthday gift. A designated flower for each month, such as, Wild Rose for January, Carnation for February, Violet for March, etc. Plain or gilt bowls. Finished in rich gray.
No. F3224   Plain Bowl
No. F3225   Gilt Bowl,

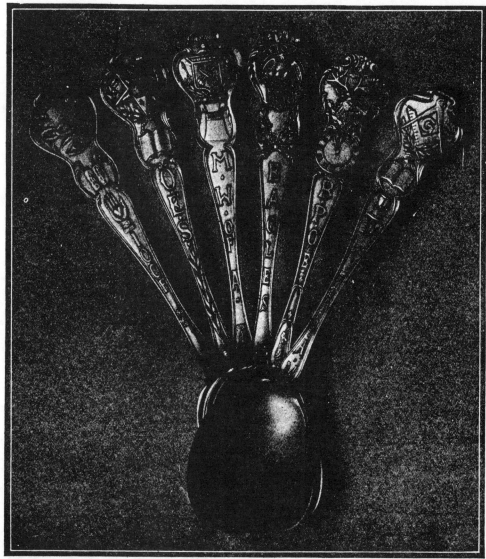

FRATERNAL SOUVENIR SPOONS

Grouped here are six fast selling Fraternal Spoons in the leading orders. Reading from left to right, they are: Odd Fellow, Eastern Star, Woodman, Eagle, Elk, and Masonic. Heavy weight, finished in rich gray with choice of plain or gilt bowls.
No. F3229   Plain Bowl
No. F3230   Gilt Bowl

STATE SOUVENIR SPOON

This same design furnished in any state of the union. It is of good weight, nicely modeled, finished in gray with choice of plain or gilt bowls. It makes a charming gift to some dear friend in distant state.
No. F3231   Plain Bowl
No. F3232   Gilt Bowl

4

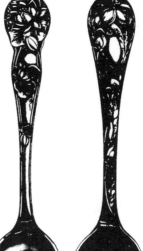

ORCHID.	IRIS.	WILD ROSE.	POND LILY.	ORANGE BLOSSOMS.	CARNATION PINK.
No. 78-4B. Large Tea.	No. 291-4B. Large Tea.	No. 292-4B. Large Tea.	No. 829-4B. Large Tea.	No. 888-4B. Large Tea.	No. 890-4B. Large Tea.
No. 78-245B. Medium Tea.	No. 291-2B. Large Coffee.	No. 292-245B. Medium Tea.	No. 829-245B. Medium Tea.	No. 888-245B. Medium Tea.	No. 890-245B. Medium Tea.
No. 78-2B. Large Coffee.		No. 292-2B. Large Coffee.	No. 829-2B. Large Coffee.	No. 888-2B. Large Coffee.	No. 890-2B. Large Coffee.

750-26N. POND LILY.
Gold Bowl -

715-26N. SWEET CLOVER.
Gold Bowl -

LITTLE BO PEEP.
724-245B. Plain
bowl,

CORN.	WHEAT.	GOLDEN ROD.	SUN FLOWER	HOLLY.
No. 442-245B. Plain	No. 522-245B. Plain	No. 475-245B. Plain	No. 516-245B. Plain	No. 571-245B. Plain

723-26N. SAGO LILY
Gold Bowl

737-26N. LILY.
Gold Bowl

5

STERLING SILVER FLORAL SOUVENIR SPOONS. GUARANTEED $\frac{925}{1000}$ FINI

French gray handles.

COLUMBINE.
No. 941-26N.
Gold bowl.

No. 941-26S.
Struck view in bowl.

COTTON BLOSSOM.
No. 520-245B. Plain
bowl,

CARNATION PINK.
No. 390-245B. Plain
bowl,

LILY OF THE VALLEY.
No. 471-245B. Plain
bowl,

FORGET ME NOT.
No. 443-245B. Plain
bowl,

TEA ROSE.
No. 513-245B. Plain
bowl,

GRAPE.
No. 944-26N.
Gold bowl,

No. 944-26S.
Struck view in bowl,

765-26N. COLUMBINE.
Gold Bowl

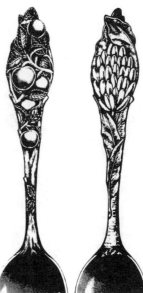

ROSE.
No. 945-26N.
Gold bowl.

No. 945-26S.
Struck view in bowl,

VIOLET.
No. 942-26N.
Gold bowl,

No. 942-26S.
Struck view in bowl,

No. 494-4. Blackberry.
size, plain bowls.
size gilt bowls.
491-245. Blackberry.
size, plain bowls.
size gilt bowls.

No. 396-4. Grapes.
Large size, plain bowls.
Large size, gilt bowls.
No. 396-245. Grapes.
Med. size, plain bowls.
Med. size, gilt bowls.

No. 476-4. Cherries.
Large size, plain bowls.
Large size, gilt bowls.
No. 476-245. Cherries.
Med. size, plain bowls.
Med. size, gilt bowls.

No. 483-4. Strawberry.
Large size, plain bowls.
Large size, gilt bowls.
No. 483-245. Strawberry.
Med. size, plain bowls.
Med. size, gilt bowls.

No. 481-4. Apple.
Large size, plain bowls.
Large size, gilt bowls.
No. 481-245. Apple.
Med. size, plain bowls.
Med. size, gilt bowls.

No. 549-4. Banana.
Large size, plain bowls.
Large size, gilt bowls.
No. 549-245. Banana.
Med. size, plain bowls.
Med. size, gilt bowls.

ORANGE BLOSSOM.
No. 7—1B Plain Bowl
No. 7—1N Gilt Bowl
Large Size.
No. 7—2B. Plain Bowl
No. 7—2N Gilt Bowl
Medium Size.

o. 488-2B. Strawberry.
Plain bowl.
o. 488-2N. Strawberry.
Gilt bowl.

No. 467-2B. Orchid.
Plain bowl.
No. 467-2N. Orchid.
Gilt bowl.

6

STERLING SILVER SOUVENIR SPOONS.
Shown Full Size.

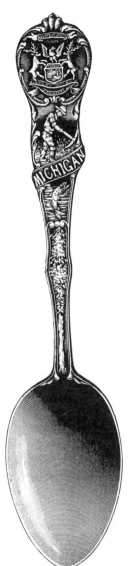

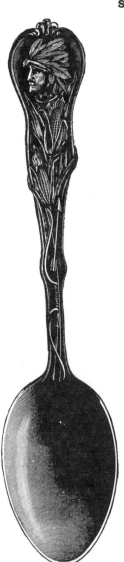

No. **5826.** State Spoon, gold bowl, (any state).

No. **5827.** Raised Indian Head, gold bowl, French gray handle..

No. **5828.** Raised figures, gold bowl, French gray handle.

No. **5829.** Raised Indian Head, gold bowl, French gray handle.

No. **5830.** Christmas Spoon, raised figures, gold bowl, French gray handle

CHRISTMAS SPOON.
No. **5832.** French gray, raised figures.

SOUVENIR SPOON. GOLD BOWL.
No. **5833.** Engraved, (any city or town in bowl as shown).
No. **5834.** Engraved, (public building) .

7

STERLING SILVER

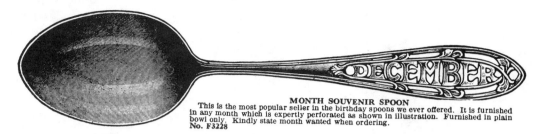

MONTH SOUVENIR SPOON
This is the most popular seller in the birthday spoons we ever offered. It is furnished in any month which is expertly perforated as shown in illustration. Furnished in plain bowl only. Kindly state month wanted when ordering.
No. F3228

LAUREL WREATH SOUVENIR SPOON
Makes a splendid gift spoon at Christening. It is artistically embossed with sufficient space for engraving. Finished in a rich gray, with choice of plain or gilt bowls.
No. F3220 Plain Bowl,
No. F3221 Gilt Bowl,

STERLING SILVER

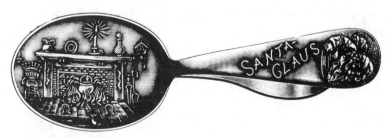

No. **5836**. State Spoon, gold bowl, raised figures, gray finish, (any state

No. **5835**. Christmas Spoon, French gray, raised figures.

French Gray Handles,

No. 350-2N. Gilt bowl,
No. 350-2S. Struck view
in bowl,

303-2N. Gilt bowl,
303-2S. Struck view in bowl,

280-4S. Struck bowl, same as cut,
280-4B. Plain bowl, medium size,

280-40B. Plain bowl, medium size,
280-2N. Gilt bowl, coffee size,

877-4S. Struck bowl, same as cut,

877-4B. Plain bowl,

245-4S. Struck bowl, same as cut,
245-4B. Plain bowl,

245-40B. Plain bowl, medium size,
245-2N. Gilt bowl, coffee size,

No. 122-245N. Gilt bowl,
engraved like cut,
No. 122-26N. Plain gilt
bowl,

303-5S. Struck bowl, same as cut,
303-40B. Plain bowl, medium size,

303-5B. Plain bowl,

282-4S. Struck bowl, same as cut,
282-4B. Plain bowl,

282-40B. Plain bowl, medium size,
282-2N. Gilt bowl, coffee size,

No. 612-245S.
Struck view in bowl,

No. 612-26N.
Plain gilt bowl,

789-40S. Struck bowl, same
as cut,

640-4S. Struck bowl, same as cut,

640-4B. Plain bowl,

No. 246-2B.
Plain bowl,

Cut showing Back of
Handle,
St. Louis City Spoon.

No. 246- 4S. Struck view in bowl, same as cut,
No. 246- 4B. Plain bowl,
No. 246- 4N. Gilt bowl,
No. 246-40B. Plain bowl, medium size,
No. 246-40N. Gilt bowl, medium size,

No. 641-4B. State Handle, plain bowl.
No. 641-4. State Handle, gilt or struck bowl,

State Handle.
No. 114-26N.
Gilt bowl.

9

French Gray Handles.

No. 11. Ark. No. 11. Ills. No. 11. Ind. No. 11. Iowa.

No. 11. Ky. No. 11. Kans. No. 11. Miss. No. 11. Mo.

No. 372-4S. Struck view in bowl like cut,
No. 372-2B. Plain bowl, Coffee Spoon,

No. 246-4N. Engraved bowl, plain script like cut,
No. 246-40B. Plain bowl, medium size,
No. 246-2N. Gilt bowl, Coffee Spoon,

No. 305-4B. Plain bowl, full size,
No. 305-40B. Plain bowl, medium size,
No. 305. Gilt bowl, Coffee Spoon,

No. 350-4B. Plain bowl, full size,
No. 350-40B. Plain bowl, medium size,

No. 251-40B. Plain bowl, medium size,
No. 251-4B. Plain bowl, full size,
No. 251-2N. Gilt bowl, Coffee Spoon,

No. 773-26S. Struck bowl, medium size,
No. 773-26B. Plain bowl, medium size,

No. 114-245S. Struck view in bowl, same as cut,
No. 114-26N. State Handle, gilt bowl,

No. 456-40S. Struck view, same as cut,
No. 456-40B. Plain bowl,

No. 456-4S. City Handle, struck view in bowl, same as cut,
No. 456-4B. City Handle, plain bowl,

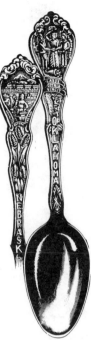

No. 11. Neb. No. 11. Okla.

No. 11. Tenn. No. 11. Texas.

STERLING SILVER BIRTHDAY, CHRISTMAS AND EASTER SOUVENIR SPOONS, GUARANTEED $\frac{925}{1000}$ FINE

FRENCH GRAY HANDLES

BUCKING BRONCO.
469-4N. Gilt
bowl,

BIRTHDAY.
No. 780-2B. ZODIAC,
plain bowl.
No. 780-2N. ZODIAC,
gold bowl,
Can furnish any month.

No. 415-4S.   Struck view in bowl, like cut,
No. 415-245S.   Five O'Clock size,

No. 832-245S. CHOIR BOY, cross and crown in bowl,
No. 832-245B. CHOIR BOY, plain bowl,
No. 832-245N. CHOIR BOY, gold bowl,

No. 472-4N.   Gold Bowl, engraved "Easter" like cut,
No. 472-4B.   Plain Bowl,
No. 472-4N.   Gold Bowl,

No. 724-245P. Etched "Merry Christmas," like cut,
No 724-245B.   Plain bowl,
No. 724-245N. Gold bowl,

No. 413-4S.   SANTA CLAUS, struck view in bowl, like cut,

No. 175-4B.   ZODIAC Birthday, plain bowl,
No. 175-4N.   ZODIAC Birthday, gold bowl,

No. 804-S-6B. Birthday
Forks,
any month

No. 393-4B.   KNIGHT OF PYTHIA, plain bowl,

No. 406-245B. COLLEGE GIRL, plain bowl, 5 O'clock size,
No. 406-4B. COLLEGE GIRL, plain bowl, full size,
No. 406-2B. COLLEGE GIRL, plain bowl, Coffee size,

No. 255-245B.
MASONIC
5 o'clock size,
plain bowl,

No. 101-245S. SANTA
CLAUS, struck view
in bowl.

No. 218-4B.
KNIGHT TEMPLAR,
large size plain bowl.

No. 175-2N. ZODIAC
Birthday Spoons
gold bowl,
Can furnish any month.

No. 615-4B.
ELK SPOON,
large size,
plain bowl,

STERLING SILVER SOUVENIR SPOONS. GUARANTEED $\frac{925}{1000}$ FINE.

French Gray Handles.

No. 52-4S. Struck view in bowl like cut,
No. 53-4B. Plain bowl,

No. 888-2B. Plain bowl,
No. 888-2N. Gilt bowl,
No. 888-2S. Struck bowl.

No. 232-4S. Struck view in bowl like cut,
No. 232-4B. Plain bowl,

No. 566-4S. Struck view in bowl like cut,
No. 566-4B. Plain Bowl,

No. 474-4N. Gilt bowl, fancy engraved, like cut,
No. 474-4B. Plain bowl,
No. 474-245B. Plain bowl,

No. 606-245B.
CHRISTIAN EN-
DEAVOR,
5 o'clock, size,
plain bowl,

No. 331-4S. Struck view in bowl, "ASCENSION,"

No. 616-245B.
EPWORTH LEAGUE
5 o'clock size,
plain bowl,

No. 414-4B. Plain bowl, Psyche handle, full size,
No. 414-245B. "   "   "   " medium size,
No. 414-2B. "   "   "   " Coffee Spoon,

GOLF PLAYER.
No. 200-4B. Plain Bowl,

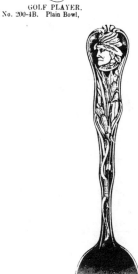

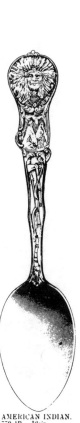

SWASTIKA.
834-245S. Struck Bow
and Arrow,

INDIAN HEAD.
202-245B. Plain

INDIAN.
422-245B. Plain

SUNNY SOUTH.
177-26N. Gilt

INDIAN HEAD.
205-26B. Plain

AMERICAN INDIAN.
770-4B. Plain
bowl,

Page 1
No. 867 - $35-45
No. 870 - $35-45
No. 868 - $35-45
No. 871 - $35-45
No. 866 - $40-50
No. 869 - $45-60
No. 943 - $35-45
No. 559 - $35-45
No. 702 - $35-45
No. 940 - $35-45
No. 475 - Toledo - $35-45
No. 11-1 - $35-45
No. 11-2 - $35-45
No. 11-3 - $35-45
No. 11-4 - $35-45
No. 11-5 - $35-45
No. 11-6 - $35-45
No. 11-7-8-9-10 - $35-45
No. 11-11 - $35-45
No. 11-12 - $35-45

Page 2
All spoons on this page average $35-45 with the exception of the following:
No. 809 - $25-30   No. 409 - Indian $80-120
No. 409 - Miner $40-50

Page 3
No. 5831 - Any month $25-35
No. 8204 - $25-35
No. 8205 - $25-35
No. 8206 - $25-35
No. 8207 - With struck bowl $30-40
No. 8208 - $15-25
No. 8209 - $15-25

Page 4
F3222-F3223 - $30-40
F3224-F3225 - $30-40
F3229-F3230 with struck bowl - $40-50
F3231-F3232 - $40-50

Page 5
All spoons on this page are $25-35 with the exception of 724 - Little Bo Peep - $40-60

Page 655-
All spoons on this page are $25-35

Page 7
No. 5826 - $35-45
No. 5827 - $35-45
No. 5828 - $35-45
No. 5829 - $35-45
No. 5830 - $35-45
No. 5832 - $35-45
No. 5833 - $35-45
No. 5834 - $35-45

Page 8
F3228 - $40-50
F3220-F3221 with struck bowl - $25-35
No. 5836 - $40-50
No. 5835 - $40-50

Page 9
All spoons on this page are $35-45 with struck bowl

Page 10
All spoons on this page are $35-45 with struck bowl
Plain bowl $25-35

Page 11
No. 469 - $25-35
No. 780 - $25-35
No. 415 - $25-35
No. 832 - $25-35
No. 872 - $30-40
No. 724 - $30-40
No. 413 - $25-35
No. 175 - $25-35
No. 501 - $25-35
No. 218 - $25-35
No. 615 - $25-35
No. 393 - $25-35
No. 406 - $30-40 with struck bowl
No. 406 plain - $30-40
No. 255 - $30-40 with struck bowl
No. 255 plain - $20-30

Page 12
No. 606 - $35-45
No. 888 - $35-45
No. 200 - $35-45
No. 53 Struck bowl - $35-45
No. 53 Plain - $30-40
No. 232 Struck bowl - $35-45
No. 232 Plain - $35-45
No. 566 Struck bowl - $35-45
No. 566 Plain - $30-40
No. 474 - $35-45
No. 616 - $35-45
No. 331 - $35-45
No. 414 - $35-45
No. 834 - $35-45
No. 202 - $35-45
No. 422 - $35-45
No. 177 - $40-60
No. 205 - $25-35
No. 770 - $35-45

Additional Spoons Not Illustrated
Abraham Lincoln - $50-60
Actress, Poli Neari - $50-60
Alaska, Cutout handle - $30-40
Alaska, Totem Pole - $30-40
Albany, N.Y., Gold Bowl, Capitol Building - $30-40
Americus - $30-40
Angeline Totem Pole, Seattle Wash. - $30-40

Army & Navy Enameled Bowl - $40-50
Atlanta - $25-35
Atlanta, IL, June 30, 1892 - $30-40
Atlantic City - $40-50
Atlantic City, NJ, Man pushing lady - $30-40
Aurora, IL Public Library - $30-50
B.P.O.E. - $30-40
Bethlehem, PA, Trombone handle - $40-50
Bibee, Arizona - $40-60
Birmingham, AL, Factory scene - $40-50
Block Island, RI, Rope handle - $30-40
Boston, Elm handle, Boston Tea Party - $45-55
Boston, Old South Church - $40-50
Boston, Paul Revere's Ride, 1775 - $40-60
Boston, Spirit of 1776, Paul Revere - $40-60
Boston Tea Party - $40-50
Bridge & Falls, Pawtucket, RI, Scene bowl - $40-50
Brockton, Mass. - $30-40
Brooklyn Bridge, N.Y. - $40-60
Buck's County Historical Society, PA - $40-60
Buffalo, N.Y., Skyline - $30-40
Bunker Hill Monument - $30-40
C.P.C., 1915, Panama Pacific Exposition - $80-90
California Cliff House in Bowl - $30-40
California Missions - $30-40
California Padre Junipero Serra - $30-40
California State, Eureka, Scenic - $30-40
California, 1915, Cutout handle - $35-45
Canada Shield - $30-40
Capitol Indianapolis, IN Gold Bowl - $30-40
Capitol Washington, D.C., Floral handle - $30-40
Capitol, Richmond, VA - $30-40
Catalina Island - $35-45
Cedar Fall, Iowa - $30-40
Charleston, S.C. - $30-40
Chatham, Ont. - $30-40
Cherokee, LA - $30-40
Chicago - $30-40
Chicago World's Fair, Whiting, Demitasse - $45-55
Chicago World's Fair - $60-70
Chicago, Enameled bowl - $75-85
Chicago, Government Building - $30-40
Chicago, IL, Skyline handle - $30-40
Chief Seattle - $30-40
Cincinnati, Ohio, Fountain in bowl - $40-50
City Hall, Birmingham, AL, Scene in bowl - $30-40
City Hall, Higginsville, MO - $30-40
City Hall, Philadelphia, PA - $30-40
Civil War Soldier, Gorham - $130-150
Cleopatra - $60-80
Cleveland, Ohio - $20-30
Cliff House, San Francisco - $30-35
Coffin House, Nantucket, Mass - $30-40
Colorado Miner, Burro Teepee, Canoe - $40-50
Colorado Springs - $20-30
Colorado Springs, Antlers Hotel - $30-40
Colorado Cripple Creek, Portland Mine - $30-40
Colorado, Lacy handle - $30-40
Columbian Exposition, Art Palace - $50-70
Columbus, Ohio, State Capitol 1899 - $30-40
Congressional Library, D.C. - $20-30
Connecticut - $30-40
Court House, Lincoln, Kansas, Scene in bowl - $30-40
Court House, Los Angeles - $30-40
Court House, Meadville, PA - $30-40

Cupid - $30-40
Darlington, Wis., Court House - $30-40
Daytona, FL - $30-40
Delaware Water Gap, PA - $20-30
Denver, Clam-Shaped Bowl - $30-40
Denver, Colo., Capitol Building in bowl - $40-60
Denver, Colorado - $30-50
Des Moines, Iowa - $30-40
Detroit - $60-80
Detroit 1903 - $60-80
Dewey Arch, NY - $30-40
Diamond Head, Honolulu, Palm Tree handle - $40-50
Duluth, Minn., Aerial bridge - $30-40
Easter Head of Man on handle - $40-50
El Paso - $30-40
Empress Hotel, Victoria, B.C. - $30-40
Evansville, IN, BPOE - $30-40
Fairfield, Iowa - $30-40
Faneuil Hall in bowl, Pilgrim on handle - $40-50
Fargo, North Dakota - $30-40
Festival Hall & Cascades, Bible handle - $40-60
Florida, enamel - $20-40
Florida, Key West - $30-40
Fond Du Lac, Wis., Rope edge - $30-40
Forman, N.D., Cutout Eagle Crest - $30-40
Fort Dearborn, 1830 - $40-50
Fort Dearborn, IL Eagle handle - $30-40
Fort Pitt, Figural handle - $30-40
Fort Sheridan - $30-40
Fort Sumter - $40-50
Fort Worth, Texas, "Lone Star" - $30-40
Freemont, Nebr. - $30-40
Garden of the God, Manitou - $30-40
Garfield Memorial Cleveland - $30-40
Georgia, Engraved bowl - $30-40
Georgia, King of the South, Bale of Cotton - $50-60
Glacier National Park - $30-40
Golden Gate, Enameled bowl - $60-70
Golden Gate, San Francisco, Bear on top - $30-40
Good Luck & Horseshoe - $30-40
Grand Canyon, AZ, Hopi Snake - $30-40
Grand Rapids, MI - $30-35
Gray's Chapel, Delaware, Ohio - $40-50
Hailey, Idaho - $30-40
Halifax, N.S. - $30-35
Hazeldenbrook, IN - $30-40
Herald Square, N.Y. - $30-40
Honolulu, Openwork - $30-40
Hook Mt., Nyack, N.Y. - $30-40
Hopi House, Grand Canyon - $40-50
Hot Springs, Ark. - $35-55
Hot Springs, Georgia - $35-55
Hotel Del Coronado - $30-50
Hutchinson, Kansas, Gilt bowl - $30-40
Idaho, State Seal Finial - $30-40
Illinois, Watson - $30-40
Independence Hall, Declaration - $40-50
Independence Hall, Liberty Bell handle - $40-50
Indian Totem Pole - $50-60
Indian with Tomahawk - $50-70
Indianapolis, Man & Buffalo handle - $40-50
Indianapolis, Soldiers & Sailors Monument - $30-40
Irish Brigade - $30-40
Ithaca, N.Y. - $30-40
Jackson, Miss. - $30-40

14

Jacksonville, FL - $40-60
Julia in bowl, Texas on handle - $30-40
Juneau - $30-40
Kansas City, Cutout handle - $20-30
Kansas City, MO, Post Office - $40-60
Kentucky - $30-35
Kramer, Indiana - $30-35
Lake Champlain - $30-35
Lake George - $30-40
Lake Tahoe - $30-40
Landing of Columbus - $40-50
Landing of the Pilgrims - $30-40
Lansing, Michigan, State Capitol - $30-40
Last Sacrifice, Niagara - $30-40
Lebanon, N.Y. - $30-40
Lenape-Penn Treaty - $30-40
Lewis-Clark Expo - $30-40
Lexington, Soldier & 1775 - $40-50
Lion's Gate Bridge, Vancouver, B.C. - $30-40
Livermore in bowl, Maine State Seal - $30-40
Long Beach, CA - $40-50
Lookout Mountain - $30-40
Lookout Mountain, Demitasse - $30-35
Los Angeles - $40-60
Louisville, KY, Gold bowl - $30-40
Lower Falls, Yellowstone Park - $30-40
Ludington, Michigan - $30-40
Luther, Martin - $30-40
Mackinac Island - $20-30
Macky Auditorium, Boulder, Colo. - $30-40
Mandan, N.D. - $30-40
Manilla - $40-60
Manitou in bowl - $30-40
Manitou, 1891 - $40-60
Maryland - $30-40
Masonic Home Chapel, Utica, N.Y. - $30-40
McCabee's Temple, Port Huron, MI - $30-40
Mexico - $30-40
Miami, FL, Figural Alligator - $30-40
Michigan - $30-40
Michigan, Bust of Indian - $30-40
Miles Standish Monument - $30-40
Milwaukee City Hall - $25-35
Mission Inn, California - $30-40
Missouri "I'm from Missouri Show Me" - $30-40
Missouri, Gold bowl - $30-40
Mobile, Alabama - $30-40
Molly Pitcher - $30-40
Montana - $30-40
Montana - $30-40
Monticello - $30-40
Montreal - $30-40
Montreal, Enamel Maple Leaf - $40-60
Montreal, Quebec, Enamel - $40-60
Montreal, Shield & Beaver - $30-40
Mount Hood - $40-50
Mount Rainier - $40-50
Mount Vernon - $30-40
Mount Washington - $30-40
Mt. Carroll - $30-40
Mt. Hood, Hood Rivers, Ore. - $30-40
Mt. Rainier, Seattle - $30-40
Mt. Rainier, Tacoma, Wash. - $40-50
Mt. Tacoma, Old Church - $30-40
Mt. Vernon - $40-50

Mt. Vernon, George Washington - $40-50
Mt. Vernon, Washington & Cherry Tree - $50-60
Muncie Normal Institute, Muncie, IN - $40-60
Muskogue - $30-40
My Old Kentucky Home - $50-60
Nantucket - $30-40
Nashville - $30-40
Navajo Indian, Figural - $40-50
Nebraska - $25-35
Negro Boy - $50-60
New Hampshire - $30-40
New Library of Congress, Capitol, D.C. - $30-40
New Mexico - $30-40
New Orleans - $25-35
New Orleans, Enameled - $40-50
New Orleans, Robert E. Lee handle - $50-60
New York City, Skyline - $40-50
New York City, Subway in Gold bowl - $30-40
New York State, Niagara Falls - $20-30
New York World's Fair - $30-40
New York, Engraved bowl - $30-40
New York, Gold bowl - $30-40
New York, N.Y., Brooklyn Bridge - $30-40
Newport News, Indian Figural - $30-40
Newport, IN - $30-40
Niagara Falls in bowl, Indian & Canoe - $40-50
Niagara Falls, Falls on handle - $40-60
Niagara, Gold bowl - $30-40
Norfolk, VA - $30-40
North Platte, Neb. - $30-40
Oil Wells, Neodesha, Kansas - $40-60
Old Ironsides, Gold bowl - $40-50
Old Point Comfort - $30-40
Old San Miguel, Santa Fe - $30-40
Osbourne Hall, Yale University - $30-40
Oshkosh, Wisconsin - $30-40
Pacific Grove, CA - $30-40
Palm Beach, Florida, Alligator handle - $40-50
Pan American Exposition - $40-50
Pan American Exposition, Ethnology Bldg. - $50-60
Pan American Exposition, Liberal Arts - $50-60
Panama Exposition, 1915, California - $50-60
Panama Exposition, San Francisco, 1915 - $40-50
Paris in bowl, Napoleon - $40-50
Pasadena, California - $40-60
Paul Revere, Bunker Hill - $30-40
Pennsylvania Depot, Piqua, Ohio - $40-60
Petoskey, Michigan - $30-40
Philadelphia, City Hall, Penn. - $30-40
Philadelphia, Gold bowl - $30-40
Philadelphia, Liberty Bell - $40-50
Philadelphia, PA - $30-40
Piedmont Hotel, Atlanta, GA - $40-50
Pike's Peak - $30-40
Pike's Peak, Colo., Cutout - $30-40
Pike's Peak, Signal Station - $30-40
Pittsburgh Skyline - $40-50
Pittsburgh, PA, Fort Pitt - $30-40
Plymouth Rock, 1620 - $40-60
Plymouth, Mass. - $30-40
Pocatello, Idaho - $30-40
Portland Observatory - $30-40
Portland, Ore., Mt. Hood in bowl - $40-60
Portland, Oregon - $30-40
Portland, Oregon, Gold bowl - $30-40

Post Office, Zanesville, Ohio - $30-40
President Washington - $30-40
Providence, R.I., Pilgrim Scene in bowl - $30-40
Providencetown, Lighthouse on handle - $40-50
Pueblo, Colorado, Wheat handle - $30-40
Rainier National Park - $30-40
Redlands, CA - $30-40
River Front, Detroit, Scene in bowl - $40-50
Riverside, CA, Gold bowl - $30-40
Rochester - $30-40
Rockford, IL Courthouse - $30-40
Rocky Mountains, Denver - $30-40
Romeo, Mich., Gold bowl - $30-40
Ruins of Jamestown, VA, Gold bowl - $40-50
Saginaw, Michigan, Elks on handle - $40-50
Salem Witch - $40-50
San Antonio, TX - $30-40
San Diego - $30-40
San Diego Mission - $30-40
San Francisco - $30-40
San Francisco Exposition - $50-60
San Gabriel Mission, California - $40-50
San Gabriel Mission, Figural handle - $40-50
San Juan, P.R. - $30-40
Santa Fe, NM - $30-40
Savannah, Georgia - $30-40
Scott County Bank, Iowa 1883-1908 - $40-50
Seattle Cutout handle - $60-80
Seattle, Chief - $30-40
Skagway, Alaska, Miner - $40-50
Sleepy Eye Flower Company - $140-160
Soldiers & Sailor's Monument, Cleveland - $40-50
Soldiers & Sailor's Monument, IN - $40-50
Soldiers & Sailor's Monument, Iowa - $30-40
Southern Pines, NC - $30-40
Spokane, Washington - $30-40
Springfield, IL, Lincoln - $30-40
St. Augustine, FL - $30-40
St. Louis World's Fair - $50-60
St. Louis World's Fair, Cascade Gardens - $50-60
St. Nicholas Church, Zanesville - $30-40
St. Paul, Minn., state Capitol - $30-40
St. Petersburg, Florida - $30-40
State Capitol, California - $40-50

State House, Boston - $30-40
Statue of Liberty - $30-40
Statue of Liberty, Tiffany - $50-70
Steamship Landing, MI - $30-40
Stockyards, Chicago, Wheat handle - $30-40
Syracuse, Engraved bowl - $30-40
T. & P. Station, Fort Worth Texas - $30-40
Tabernacle, Salt Lake City - $40-50
Tacoma, Chief Tacoma on handle - $40-50
Teddy Roosevelt - $40-60
The Golden Gate, San Francisco - $40-50
The New York Press Club, Embossed Owl - $40-50
The White House, Washington, D.C. - $40-50
Thousand Islands - $40-50
Times Square, Broadway, N.Y. - $30-40
Totem Pole - $40-60
Trenton, N.J., 1776 in bowl - $30-40
Union Station, St. Louis, MO - $40-50
Utah - $30-40
Utah, Mormon Temple in bowl - $30-40
Valley City, N.D., Gold bowl - $30-40
Valley Forge - $30-40
Vancouver, Canada - $30-40
Vassar College - $40-50
Victoria, B.C., Gold bowl - $30-40
Virginia-SS - $30-40
Washington State, Bust of Washington - $30-40
Washington's Tomb - $30-40
Washington, D.C., Capitol Finial - $30-40
Washington, D.C., Cutout - $40-50
Washington, D.C., Eagle & Capitol in bowl - $30-40
Washington, D.C., Gold Bowl - $30-40
Watertown, NY - $30-40
Wilkes Barre, PA, Gold bowl - $30-40
William Penn, Independence Hall - $30-40
Williamsburg, VA - $30-40
Wisconsin, State Capitol - $40-60
Woman's Building, Columbian - $50-60
World's Columbian Exposition - $50-60
World's Fair, 1893 - $55-65
Wyoming - $30-40
Yale, 1893 - $40-50
Yellowstone Park - $30-40
Yonkers, NY - $30-40
Zodiac, All Months - $25-35

PRICES ON EBAY MAY BE MUCH HIGHER DUE TO LOCAL INTEREST.

Price Guide

The prices in this book have been arrived at by averaging out the items offered for sale throughout various trade papers, auctions, flea markets, antique shows and private dealers. These prices are only a guide as they may vary from one region to another.

Remember, this is only a guide. We are not in the business of buying or selling merchandise in this book.

STERLING SILVER CHILD'S SETS AND BABY SPOONS.

Child's Spoon.   Gold Lined Bowl.
No. **8201**

Child's Spoon.   Gold Lined Engraved Bowl.
No. **8202** .

Child's Spoon.   Gold Lined Engraved Bowl.
No. **8203**

No. **5819**.   Etched bowl.

No. **5820**.   Etched bowl

No. **5818**. Etched bowl.
each .

No. **5821**.   Etched bowl.

No. **5822**.   Etched bowl.

No. **5823**. Child Spoon,
French gray, engrav-
ed bowl,

No. **5825**. Child Spoon,
French gray, engrav-
ed, bowl,

15

Solid Sterling Silver

BABY SPOON
Sol'd Sterl'ng Silver. Celebrated Brandon pattern. Bent Handle. Br.ght finish. Our pr.ce is very low. (Cut actual s.ze).
No. B3303

BABY SPOON
Solid Sterl'ng S lver. The Beautiful Devonsh're pattern. Bent handle. French gray fin sh. Extra weight. (Cut actual s'ze.)
No. B3304

BABY SPOON
Sol'd Sterl'ng S!lver. Bent handle. French gray fin sh. Appropriate space for engrav.ng. (Cut actual s.ze.)
No. B3305

BABY SPOON
Sol'd Sterl ng Silver. Bent handle. Embossed de-s!gn which interests the baby. Gray finish. (Cut actual s ze.)
No. B3306

BABY SPOON
Solid Sterling Silver. Decorated bent handle. Me-dium weight. Gray finish. Attractively priced in this selling. (Cut actual size).
No. B3301

BABY SPOON
Solid Sterl'ng S'lver. Bent handle. Fancy struck bowl and handle. Subjects clearly defined. French gray finish. (Cut actual size).
No. B3302

No. 5815. Gold bowl,

BABY FORK
French Gray Finish.
No. F3218
Also furnished in spoon to match.
No. F3219

BABY SPOON
Gray Finish.
No. F3226
Also furnished in fork to match.
No. F3227

16

STERLING SILVER NAPKIN RINGS AND CHILD'S CUPS $\frac{925}{1000}$ FINE.

No. B 10   Engraved, gold lined....

No. B 22   Engraved, gold lined....

No. B 32   Engraved, gold lined....

No. B 013   Plain, gold lined.......

No. B 28   Sterling Napkin Ring...

No. B 11   Satin engraved, gold lined

No. B 12 Satin engraved, gold lined

No. B 25   Cup, plain, gold lined.

No. B 49   Sterling Napkin Ring.

No. B 22   Cup, satin, B. C., engraved,
    gold lined ----------------------

No. B 015   Plain, gold lined..

No. B 20   Cup, satin, B. C., engraved,
    gold lined................

No. C1920   Tea Strainer.

No. C192   Napkin Ring
Actual size.

No. C1321   Gravy Boat, gilt.   Length, 7½ in.

No. C1676   Mustard Pot,

No. C207   Napkin Ring,
Actual size.

No. C1678   Mustard Pot

No. C173   Puff Box.

No. C204   Napkin Ring,
Actual size.

No. C509   Puff Box

No. C11   Tea Caddy,
Height, 4 inches.

No. C213   Flask,

No. C1464   Atomizer.

No. C1735   Claret Jug,

Sterling Silver Trimmed Combs.

Ladies' Ebonoid Comb.   Sterling Silver Trimmed.
No. **7087** .

Gent's Ebonoid Comb.   Sterling Silver Mounting.
No. **7088** .

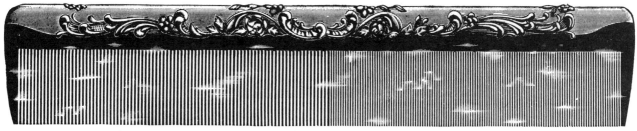

Ladies' Sterling Silver Trimmed Comb.
No. **7089** .

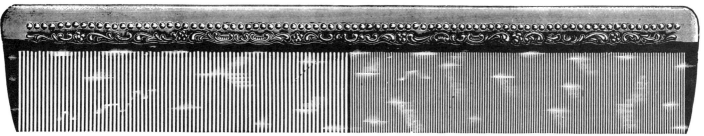

Ladies' Large Size Sterling Silver Trimmed Comb.
No. **7090** .

Ladies' Large Size Sterling Silver Trimmed Comb.
No. **7091**

Ladies' Large Size Sterling Silver Trimmed Comb.
No. **7092** .

Sterling Silver Toiletware

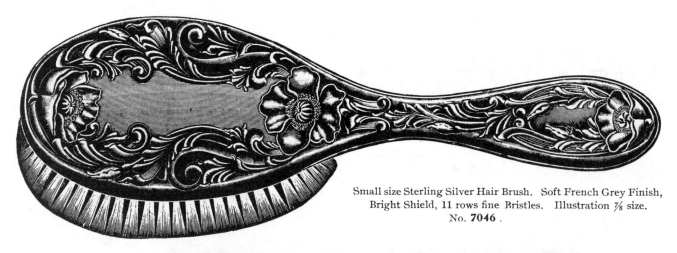

Small size Sterling Silver Hair Brush. Soft French Grey Finish, Bright Shield, 11 rows fine Bristles. Illustration ⅞ size. No. **7046**.

No. **5350**. Sterling silver Clothes Brush, heavily Mounted, French gray finish, length 7½ inches.

No. **5333**. Cloth Brush, 7 inches long.

No. **5337**. Military Brush, 4½ inches long.

No. **5484**. Bonnet Brush, French gray finish, length 8½ inches.

STERLING SILVER TOILET WARE

Extra Heavy Sterling Silver Hair Brush. Raised Ornamentation, Soft, Grey Finish, 15 Rows Extra Fine Bristles. Illustration ⅞ size.

No. **7039** .

No. **5345**. Sterling silver Hair Brush, heavily mounted, French gray, length 8¾ inches.

No. **5341**. Hair Brush, 8 inches.

No. **5349**. Sterling silver Military Brush. French gray finish, heavily mounted, length 4½ inches.

Sterling Silver Mirror.

Small Size Hand
Mirror.
Sterling Silver
Trimmed, French
Grey Finish.
Illustration full size.
No. 7056.

No. 5347. Sterling silver Mirror, heavily mounted, French gray
finish, diameter of glass 4¾ inches.

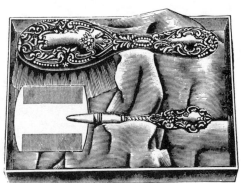

Child's Set. Comb and Brush; Sterling Silver
Trimmed;
No. 7052 .

Sterling Silver Mirror.

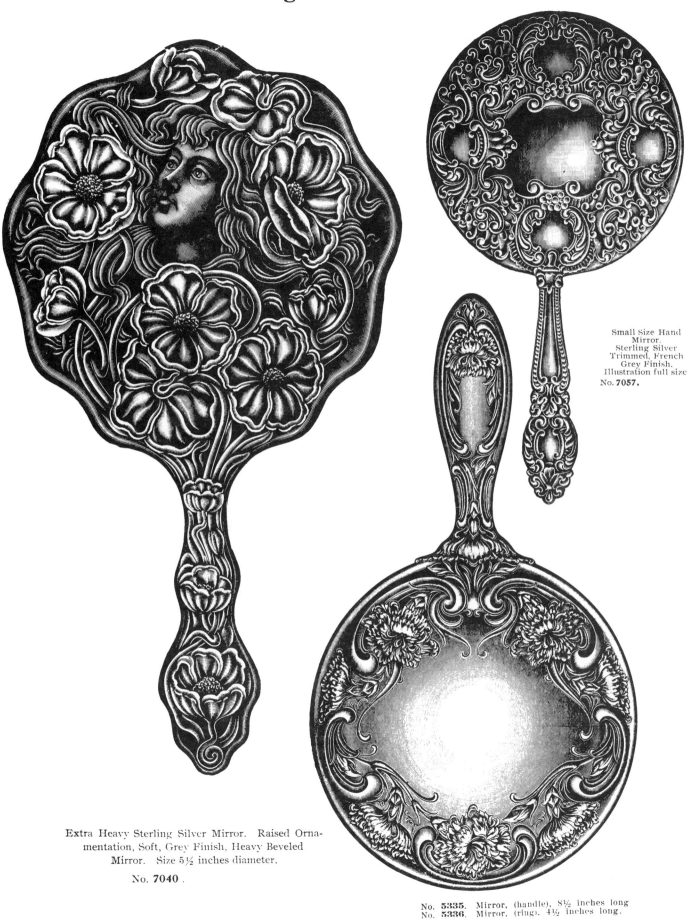

Small Size Hand Mirror. Sterling Silver Trimmed, French Grey Finish. Illustration full size No. **7057.**

Extra Heavy Sterling Silver Mirror. Raised Ornamentation, Soft, Grey Finish, Heavy Beveled Mirror. Size 5½ inches diameter.

No. **7040** .

No. **5335.** Mirror, (handle), 8½ inches long
No. **5336.** Mirror, (ring), 4½ inches long.

23

STERLING SILVER BRUSHES

Sterling Silver Cloth Brush. Extra heavy raised ornamented back, soft grey finish,
No. **7036**.

No. **5485**. Whisk Broom, sterling silver handle and cape, length 9 inches.

No. **5486**. Hair Whisk Broom, sterling silver mounting, length 6 inches .

Sterling Silver Military Brush.
soft grey finish,
No. **7034**.

STERLING SILVER TOILET WARE,

Illustrations are about
⅔ actual size.

Manufactured and
Guaranteed by
Simpson, Hall,
Miller & Co.

No. B10   Mirror, length 13 inches,
No. B11   Hair Brush, length 10 inches,
No. B12   Ladies' Comb. length 7¾ inches.

25

Solid Sterling Silver Toiletware

Manufactured and Guaranteed by
Simpson, Hall, Miller and Co.

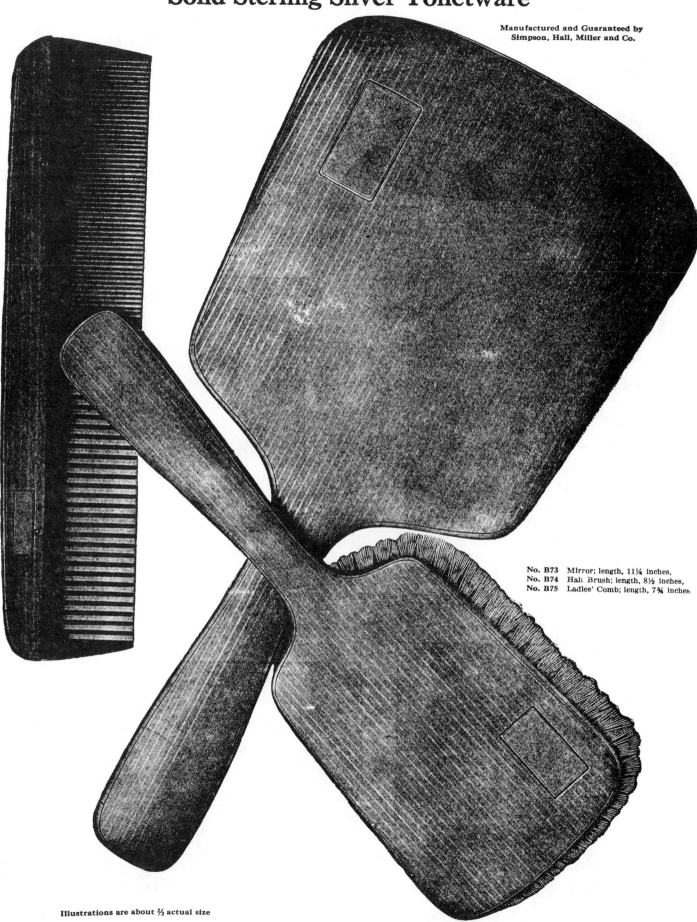

No. B73   Mirror; length, 11¼ inches.
No. B74   Hair Brush; length, 8½ inches.
No. B75   Ladies' Comb; length, 7¾ inches.

Illustrations are about ⅔ actual size

Sterling Silver Toiletware

Illustrations are about ⅔
actual size.

**Manufactured and
Guaranteed by
Simpson, Hall,
Miller & Co.**

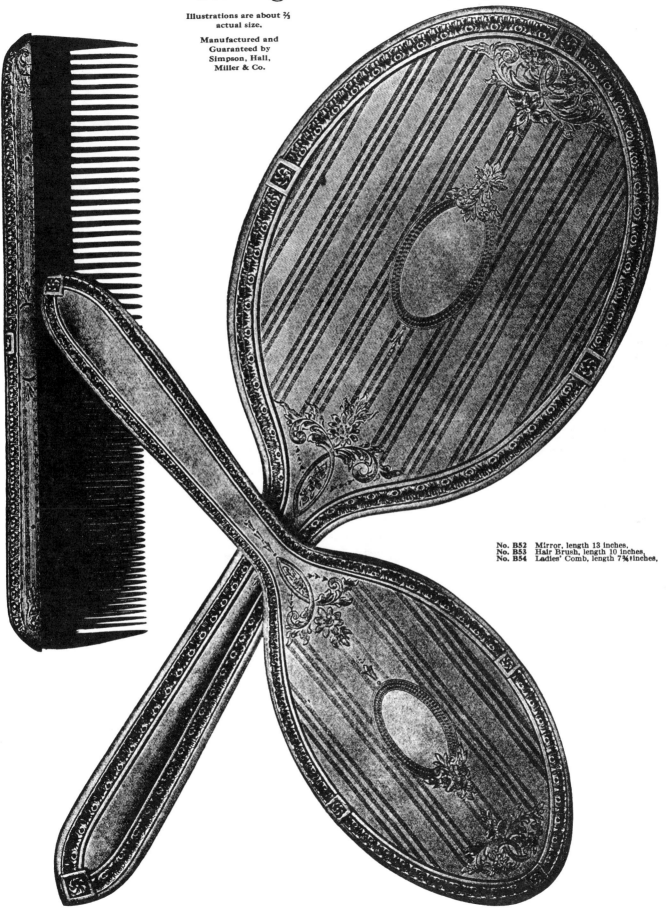

No. B52   Mirror, length 13 inches,
No. B53   Hair Brush, length 10 inches,
No. B54   Ladies' Comb, length 7¾ inches,

Sterling Silver Handle Manicure and Library Articles.

ILLUSTRATIONS FULL SIZE.

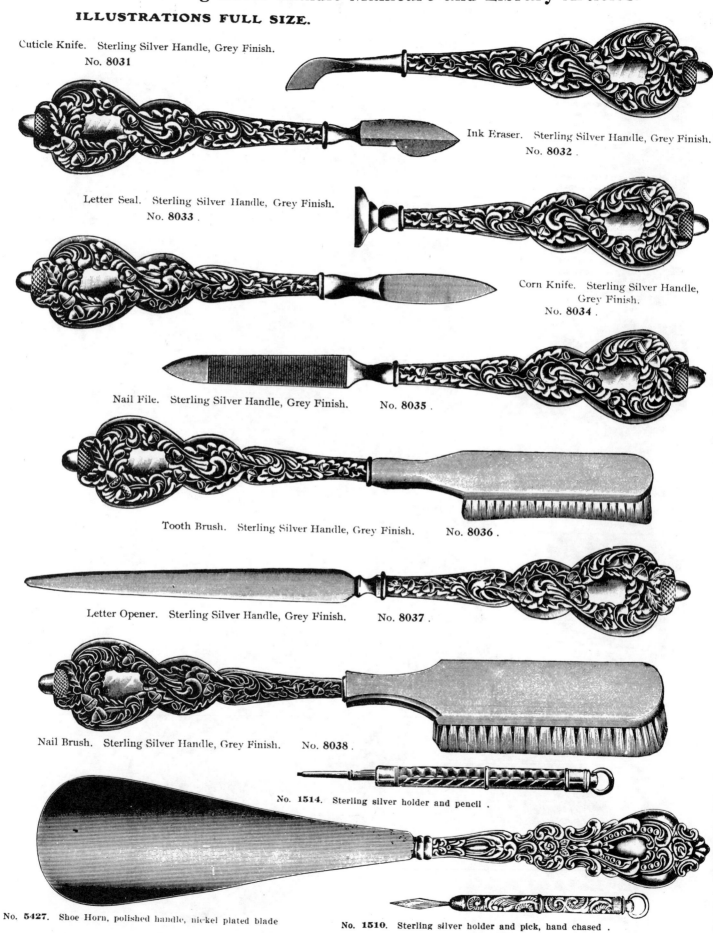

Cuticle Knife.   Sterling Silver Handle, Grey Finish.
No. 8031

Ink Eraser.   Sterling Silver Handle, Grey Finish.
No. 8032 .

Letter Seal.   Sterling Silver Handle, Grey Finish.
No. 8033 .

Corn Knife.   Sterling Silver Handle,
Grey Finish.
No. 8034 .

Nail File.   Sterling Silver Handle, Grey Finish.   No. 8035 .

Tooth Brush.   Sterling Silver Handle, Grey Finish.   No. 8036 .

Letter Opener.   Sterling Silver Handle, Grey Finish.   No. 8037 .

Nail Brush.   Sterling Silver Handle, Grey Finish.   No. 8038 .

No. 1514.   Sterling silver holder and pencil .

No. 5427.   Shoe Horn, polished handle, nickel plated blade

No. 1510.   Sterling silver holder and pick, hand chased .

28

STERLING SILVER MANICURE SETS.

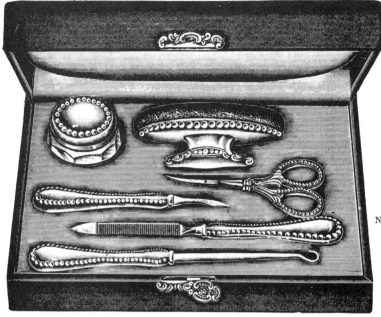

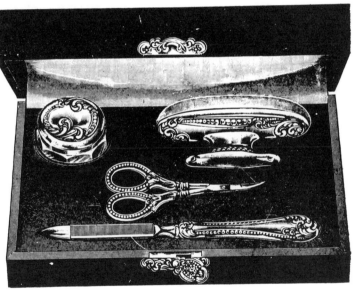

No. **5319**. Manicure Set, 4 pieces, sterling silver mountings, in silk lined case, cut one-half size.

No. **5320**. Sterling silver, 6 piece Manicure Set, in silk lined box, length 8½ inches.

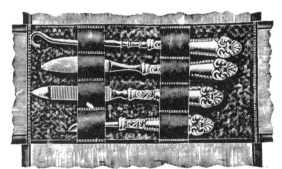

No. **5323**. Manicure Set, in folding leather case, sterling silver mountings, cut one-half size.

No. **5324**. Sterling silver, 4 piece Manicure Set, in silk box, length 8 inches .

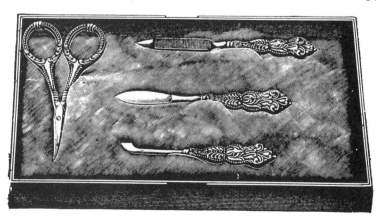

No. **5321**. Manicure Set, in silk lined case, sterling silver mounttings, cut one-half size.

Solid Sterling Silver Vanity Cases

DORINE HOLDER
Solid Sterling silver; richly engine turned; octagonal design; contains mirror, powder placque and puff; height ½ inch.
No. T245-1-5

VANITY CASE
Artistically engine turned and beautifully hand engraved with shield for monogram.
No. T741/203

DORINE HOLDER
Solid Sterling silver; masterly hammered; contains mirror, powder placque and puff; height ⅜ inch.
No. T249H

VANITY CASE
Rich engine turned design with magnificent hand engraved borders and a lovely center shield for monogram.
No. T741/135

DORINE HOLDER
Solid Sterling silver; rich engine turned design; contains mirror, powder placque and puff; height ⅜ inch.
No. T229-1-8

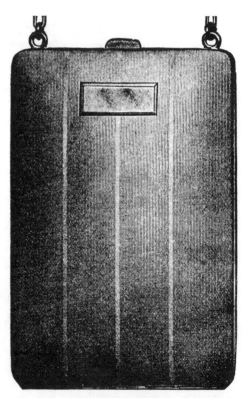

VANITY CASE
Rich engine turned design with shield for engraving.
No. T741/1/8

Shaving Sets

No. **6433**. Shaving Set, burnished, gold lined .

Shaving Brush. Sterling Silver Handle, Bright Finish.
No. **8001** .

No. **5488**. Sterling silver Shaving Brush, full size.

Shaving Brush. Sterling Silver Handle, French Grey Finish.
No. **8000** .

No. **5489**. Sterling silver handle, fine steel blade, length 6 inches.

STERLING SILVER

No. **5490**. Sterling silver mounted Shaving Brush, full size.

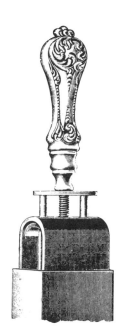

No. **5487**. Razor Strop, sterling silver handle, length 12 inches .

No. **6437**. Tissue Soap Box. nickel silver.

No. **6435**. Shaving Set, satin shield, gold lined .

31

Sterling Silver Handle Manicure and Library Articles. French Grey Finish.

ILLUSTRATIONS FULL SIZE.

Ink Eraser. Sterling Silver Handle,
French Grey Finish.
No. **8021** .

Cuticle Knife. Sterling Silver Handle,
French Grey Finish.
No. **8022** .

Corn Knife. Sterling Silver Handle,
French Grey Finish.
No. **8023** .

Letter Seal. Sterling Silver Handle, French Grey Finish.
No. **8024** .

Button Hook. Sterling Silver Handle, French Grey Finish.   No. **8025** .

Nail File. Sterling Silver Handle, French Grey Finish.   No. **8026**

Curler. Sterling Silver Handle, French Grey Finish.   No. **8027** .

Paper Cutter. Metal Blade, Sterling Silver Handle, French Grey Finish.   No. **8028** .

Tooth Brush. Sterling Silver Handle, French Grey Finish.   No. **8029** .

Paper Cutters, Roll Blotters and Darners, Sterling Silver Handle.

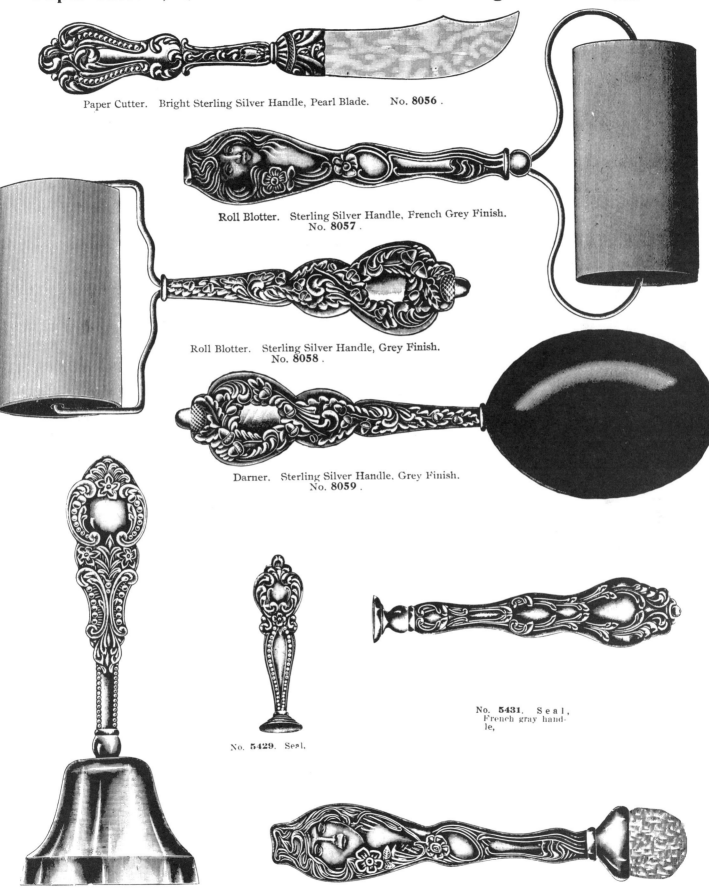

Paper Cutter. Bright Sterling Silver Handle, Pearl Blade. No. **8056**.

Roll Blotter. Sterling Silver Handle, French Grey Finish. No. **8057**.

Roll Blotter. Sterling Silver Handle, Grey Finish. No. **8058**.

Darner. Sterling Silver Handle, Grey Finish. No. **8059**.

No. **5429**. Seal.

No. **5431**. Seal, French gray handle,

No. **5430**. Call Bell, sterling silver handle, nickel plated bell.

No. **5433**. Stamp Moistener, sterling silver handle, French gray finish.

STERLING SILVER SEWING SETS.
EMERY BALLS AND SCISSORS.

No. 25

No. **5451**. Sterling Silver Sewing Set, 5 pieces, cased in leatherette velvet lined box, shown one-half size

No. **5452**. Needle Emery, sterling silver mounted.

No. **5453**. Needle Emery, sterling silver mounted.

No. **5457**. Needle Emery, sterling silver mounted.

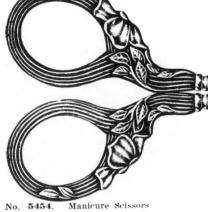

No. **5454**.   Manicure Scissors

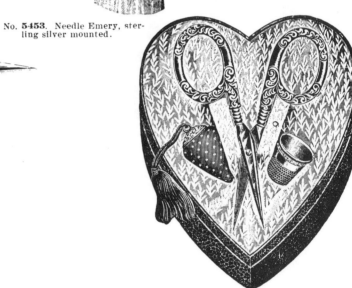

No. **5456**.   Sewing Set, 3 pieces, thimble, scissors and emery ball, in paper box, with cover, illustration one-half size,

No. **5462**.   Sewing Scissors, sterling silver handle, shown full size.

No. **5460**.   Manicure Scissors, sterling silver handles.
No. **5461**.   Embroidery Scissors, sterling silver handles.
Shown Full Size.

Sterling Silver Bag Checks

Bag Check. Sterling Silver, **French G**rey Finish, Leather Strap.
No. 8107 .

Bag Check. Sterling Silver, French Grey Finish, Leather Strap.
No. 8108 .

Bag Check. Sterling Silver, Satin Finish, Leather Strap.
No. 8109 .

Bag Check. Sterling Silver, Bright Finish, Leather Strap.
No. 8110 .

STERLING SILVER THIMBLES.

No. **1240**. Sterling silver,

No. **1241**. Sterling silver,

No. **1242**. Sterling silver,

No. **1243**. Sterling silver,

No. **1244**. Sterling silver,

No. **1245**. Sterling silver,

No. **1246**. Sterling silver,

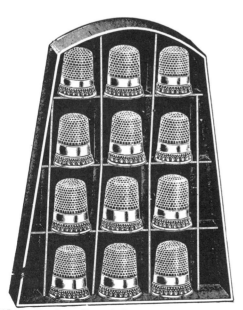

No. **1247**. Sterling silver, 1 dozen assorted, put up in paper box .

No. **1248**. Sterling silver, open top.

No. **1239**

No. **1234**. Sterling silver,

No. **1235**. Sterling silver,

No. **1236**. Sterling silver,

No. **1237**. Sterling silver,

No. **1238**. Sterling silver,

Sterling Silver Match Boxes

Match Box. Heavy Sterling Silver.
French Grey Finish. No. 8156

Match Box. Heavy Sterling Silver.
French Grey Finish. No. 8157

Match Box. Heavy Sterling Silver.
French Grey Finish. No. 8158

Match Box. Heavy Sterling Silver.
French Grey Finish. No. 8159

Match Box. Sterling Silver, French
Grey Finish. No. 8160

Match Box. Sterling Silver, Satin Finish.
No. 8161

Match Box. Sterling Silver, Bright Finish.
No. 8162

Match Box. Sterling Silver, French
Grey Finish. No. 8163

Match Box. Sterling Silver, Bright Finish.
No. 8164

Match Box. Sterling Silver, French
Grey Finish. No. 8165

Match Box. Sterling Silver, Bright Finish.
No. 8166

Match Box. Sterling Silver, Satin Finish.
No. 8167

36

STERLING SILVER MATCH BOXES.

Shown Full Size.

No. **5860.** Raised figure, French gray, gold lined, extra heavy

No. **5859.** Raised Indian head

No. **5862.** The Elk Match Safe, heavy embossed design

No. **5863.** Embossed, gray finish

No. **5870.** Polished, embossed

No. **5864.** Plain polished, beaded, gold lined

No. **5868.** Polished, raised embossed border, gold lined

No. **5861.** Raised figure, French gray

No. **5869.** Satin finished, embossed

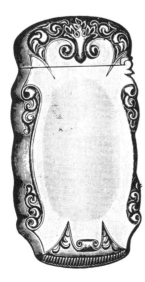

No. **5866.** Raised border, French gray, gold lined

No. **5867.** Burnished, raised border, gold lined

No. **5865.** Embossed, French gray finish

Solid Sterling Silver Cigarette Cases and Match Boxes

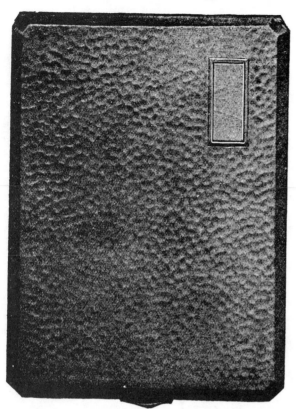

CIGARETTE CASE

Thin Model.   Beveled Edges.   Single Row.

An attractive design that is masterly hammered. Shield for monogram. Interior nicely damaskeened and finished in a rich golden color.

No. T92H

CIGARETTE CASE

Thin Model.   Beveled Edges.   Single Row.

An artistic engine turned design. Shield for monogram. Interior elegantly damaskeened and finished in a rich golden color.

No. TS2/27

MATCH BOX

Solid sterling silver. Rich engine turned design. Space for monogram. Ring at top to attach to chain. (Holds paper matches). Gold interior beautifully damaskeened.

No. T40/27

MATCH BOX

Solid sterling silver. Rich hammered design. Space for monogram. Ring at top to attach to chain. (Holds paper matches.) Gold interior, beautifully damaskeened.

No. T66H

MATCH BOX

Solid sterling silver. Rich engine turned design. Heavy weight. Shield for monogram.

No. T58/55

Solid Sterling Silver Cigarette Cases

ILLUSTRATIONS ARE ACTUAL SIZE

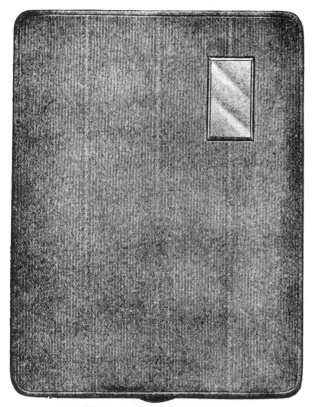

BOOK MODEL SINGLE ROW CIGARETTE CASE
Solid Sterling Silver. Thin Model. Gold Lined Damaskeened Interior. Monogram. Richly Engine Turned Design.
No. T85-201

BOOK MODEL SINGLE ROW CIGARETTE CASE
Solid Sterling Silver. Thin Model. Gold Lined Damaskeened Interior. Monogram. Richly Engine Turned Design.
No. T85-197

14K INLAID GOLD STRIPED CIGARETTE CASE
This DE LUXE cigarette case is made of Solid Sterling Silver, extra weight. Thin Model single row case. Magnificent Engine Turned design, with attractive GREEN AND RED GOLD STRIPES, making it very prepossessing in appearance. Shield for Monogram. Interior beautifully damaskeened in a rich golden color. Finest degree of expert workmanship and finish.
No. T1082-213

14K INLAID GOLD STRIPED CIGARETTE CASE

No. T1391-12

39

STERLING SILVER

Sterling Silver Soap Box. Bright Finish.
No. 8931 .

No. **5886**. Salt Set, consisting of two Salt Cellars and two Spoons, gold lined, cased in satin lined box, (illustration two-third size).

Stamp Box. Sterling Silver,
No. **8169** .

Stamp Box. Sterling Silver,
No. **8168** .

No. **5366**. Cut glass Pungent, sterling silver mounted .

No. **5367**. Sterling silver mounted cut glass Pungent.
Cut full size.

No. **5369**. Nail Polisher, sterling silver mounting, length 4½ inches.

Coat Mark and Hanger. Sterling Silver.
No. **8096** .

No. **5371**. Nail Polisher, sterling silver mounting, French gray finish, cut full size .

Coat Hanger. Sterling Silver, Grey Finish.
No. **8094** .

Solid Sterling Silver Flasks

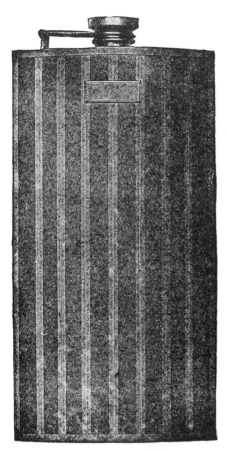

THE JULIET PERFUME FLASK

(Actual Size)

A thin Flat Flask in Solid Sterling Silver. Finished as beautiful as an exquisite watch case. The stopper is equipped with a long dropper. Novel. Graceful. Convenient.

No. RNT3155

STERLING SILVER FLASK

Solid Sterling Silver. Very heavy weight. Square shape and bottom. Will stand erect. Decided concaved back perfectly fitting the "hip." Patented top. Unusually well made and unsurpassed in finish. A very distinctive and high quality flask. Choice of hammered design as shown or perfectly plain as quoted below, with choice of three capacities, viz.: ½, ¾ or the full pint.

CAPACITY, ½ PINT
Height, 5⅞ inches; width, 4¼ inches
No. T852H Hammered Design,
No. T852P Plain Design,

CAPACITY, ¾ PINT
Height, 7⅜ inches; width, 4¼ inches
No. T853H Hammered Design.
No. T853P Plain Design.

CAPACITY, 1 PINT
Height, 8⅜ inches; width, 4¾ inches
No. T854H Hammered Design,
No. T854P Plain Design,

STERLING SILVER FLASK.

Solid Sterling Silver. Very heavy weight. Square shape and bottom. Will stand erect. Decided concaved back perfectly fitting the "hip." Patented top. The finest degree of mastership construction is discernible throughout. The finish is unsurpassed. Choice of a most exquisite engine turned design as shown or a perfectly plain pattern as quoted below. Choice of ½, ¾ or the full pint capacities.

CAPACITY, ½ PINT
Height, 5⅞ inches; width, 4¼ inches
No. T852/27 Engine Turned Design
No. T852P   Plain Design,

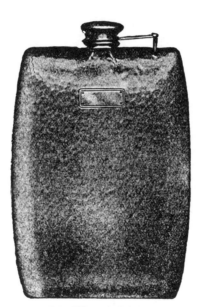

STERLING SILVER FLASK
(Watrous Silver Co.)

Solid Sterling Silver. Heavy weight. Masterly constructed and elegantly finished. Rounded corners, knife edges, concaved back. Patented top. Choice of masterly hammered design as shown or perfectly plain pattern as quoted below in both the ½ or ¾-pint capacities.

CAPACITY, ½ PINT
Height, 6 inches; width, 4 inches
No. T855H Hammered design,
No. T855P Plain design,

CAPACITY, ¾ PINT
Height, 7½ inches; width, 4¾ inches
No. T856H Hammered design,
No. T856P Plain design,

PERFUME FLASK

(Actual Size)

A dainty Perfume Flask made of Solid Sterling Silver and equipped with a long dropper. A useful and beautiful novelty for milady's hand bag. Rich engine turned design with space for engraving.

No. R3275ET

STERLING SILVER FLASK
(Watrous Silver Co.)
(Illustration one-third size)

Solid sterling silver. Heavy weight. Made and finished exceptionally well. Capacity, ⅛ pint. Choice of engine turned (as illustrated) or perfectly plain or hammered as quoted below.

No.	Style
T863/167ET	Engine turned.
T863/167P	Perfectly plain.
T863/167H	Hammered.

PERFUME FLASK

(Actual Size)

Solid Sterling Silver. Enamelled both sides. Long dropper. Exquisite design. Moderately priced. Choice of Blue or Pink Hard French Enamelled colors.

No. R3216

Whiskey Flasks.

STERLING SILVER

Flask. Embossed Burnished.
Illustration one-half size.
No. 8881.

No. 6610. Flask, satin engraved, ½ size.

Sterling Silver Flask. Embossed French Grey
Finish. Illustration full size.
No. 8882.

No. 6609. Flask, satin engraved, ½ size.

No. 6608. Flask, satin engraved, collapsion
cup, gold lined.

Baby Rattles, Bib Chains and Key Rings.
STERLING SILVER

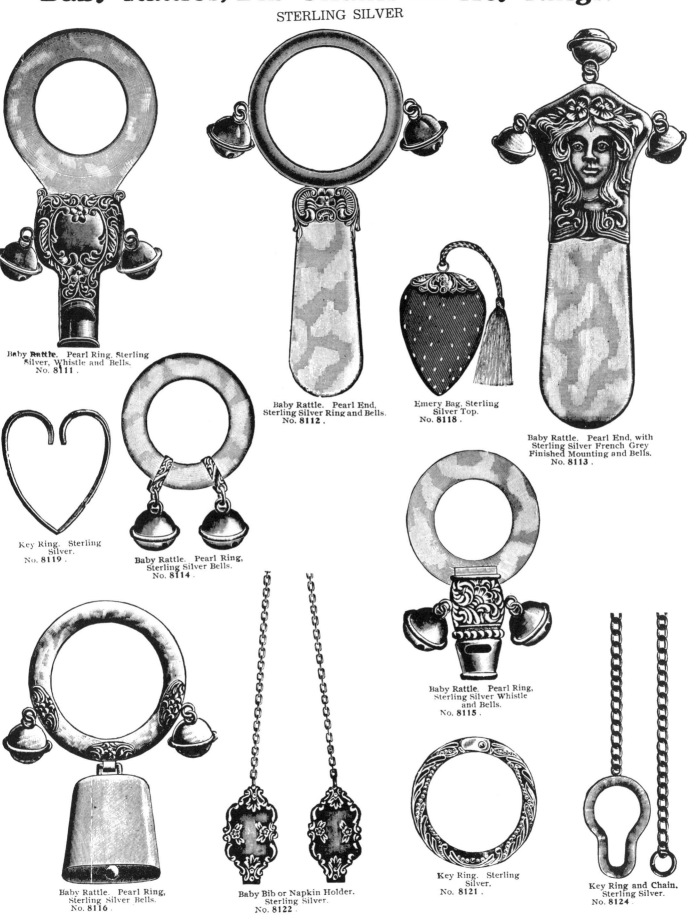

Baby Rattle. Pearl Ring. Sterling
Silver, Whistle and Bells.
No. 8111 .

Baby Rattle. Pearl End,
Sterling Silver Ring and Bells.
No. 8112 .

Emery Bag, Sterling
Silver Top.
No. 8118 .

Baby Rattle. Pearl End, with
Sterling Silver French Grey
Finished Mounting and Bells.
No. 8113 .

Key Ring. Sterling
Silver.
No. 8119 .

Baby Rattle. Pearl Ring,
Sterling Silver Bells.
No. 8114 .

Baby Rattle. Pearl Ring,
Sterling Silver Whistle
and Bells.
No. 8115 .

Baby Rattle. Pearl Ring,
Sterling Silver Bells.
No. 8116 .

Baby Bib or Napkin Holder.
Sterling Silver.
No. 8122 .

Key Ring. Sterling
Silver.
No. 8121 .

Key Ring and Chain.
Sterling Silver.
No. 8124 .

Solid Sterling Silver Napkin Rings

NAPKIN RING (S. H. M. & CO.)
Magnificently hand engraved.   Bright finish.   Heavy
weight. Cut actual size. **No. B3323**

NAPKIN RING (WATROUS)
Richly engine turned and engraved. Gold lined. Bright
or gray finish. Heavy weight. Cut actual size.
No. T3325

NAPKIN RING (S. H. M. & CO.)
Engine turned and engraved. Bright finish.   Circlet for
engraving. Heavy weight. Cut actual size.
No. B3324

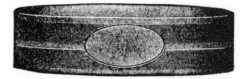

NAPKIN RING (S. H. M. & CO.)
Engine turned, engraved shield, bright finish, cut actual
size.
No. B3322

NAPKIN RING (WATROUS)
Perfectly plain; bright finish; cut actual
size.
No. T3326

NAPKIN RING (WATROUS)
Perfectly plain; bright finish; cut actual
size.
No. T3328

NAPKIN RING (WATROUS)
Richly engine turned; shield for engraving;
bright or gray finish; cut actual size.
No. T3327

NAPKIN RING
Reproduction of Dutch Silver; raised design;
height, 1½ inches; diameter, 1½ inches.
No. 1A2-60

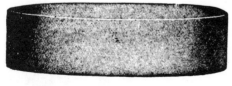

NAPKIN RING (S. H. M. & CO.)
Perfectly plain. Cut exact size. **No. B3320**

NAPKIN RING (S. H. M. & CO.)
Hand hammered, chased shield. Gray finish. Cut exact
size.
No. B3321

NAPKIN RING (WATROUS)
Pierced design; bright finish; cut actual
size.
No. T3329

44

No. **6529**. Napkin Ring, satin B. C.,

No. **6528**. Napkin Ring, satin engraved,

Napkin Ring. Satin Engraved No. **8783**

No 2105.

No. 2106.

No. **1A2X21** Napkin Ring,

No. **1A2-45** Napkin Ring,

No. **1A2-55** Napkin Ring,

No. 2108.

No. **2109**.

No. **6524**. Napkin Ring, burnished,

No. **6525**. Napkin Ring, satin B. C.,

No. **6526**. Napkin Ring, satin engraved,

NAPKIN RINGS.

No. **6535**. Napkin Ring, chased.

No. **6536**. Napkin Ring,

No. **6537**. Napkin Ring.

No. **6538**. Napkin Ring,

Napkin Ring. Engraved.
No. **8776**

No. **6523**. Napkin Ring, burnished,

Napkin Ring. Bright Chased.
No. **8781**

Napkin Ring. Bright Chased
No. **8784**

Illustrations Full Size.

No. **6534**. Napkin Ring, satin engraved,

No. **6532**. Napkin Ring, satin B. C..

No. **6533**. Brownie Napkin Ring, bright cut. Brownies in colors,

No. **6530**. Napkin Ring, burnished.

Napkin Ring. Satin Engraved, Triple Plated. No. **8782**

No. **6527**. Satin engraved.

Napkin Ring. Burnished.
No. **8778**

No. **6531**. Satin engraved,

NAPKIN RINGS.

No. **6494**. Napkin Ring, satin, B. C., gold lined

No. **6510**. Napkin Ring, burnished,

No. **6501**. Napkin Ring, satin engraved, full size

No. **6498**. Napkin Ring, satin B. C., full size

STERLING SILVER

No. **6497**. Napkin Ring, silver, full size,

No. **6502**. Napkin Ring, satin engraved, illustration full size

No. **6500**. Napkin Ring, satin engraved.

Napkin Ring. Satin Engraved, Gold Lined.
No. **8774**

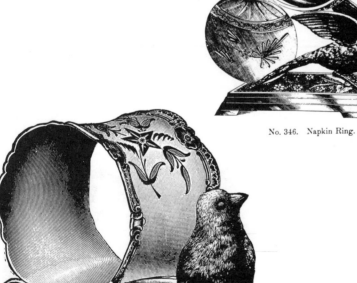

No. 346.   Napkin Ring.

Napkin Ring. Satin Engraved.
No. **8775**

No. **6496**. Napkin Ring, satin B. C., full
size

Solid Sterling Silver Salts and Peppers and Salt Sets

SALT AND PEPPER SET
(S. H. M. & Co.)
Bright finish. Height 3½ inches.
Lined paper box. Cork aperture at
bottom. A charming octagonal Colonial design.
No. B3470

SALT AND PEPPER SET
(S. H. M. & Co.)
Bright finish. Height, 3½ inches. Octagonal design. Cork aperture at bottom.
Encased in the richest gray silk lined cabinet
made.
No. B3471

SALT AND PEPPER SET IN GIFT CASE
(S. H. M. & Co.)
Bright finish. Height, 5¼ inches. Cork aperture at bottom.
Encased in an elaborate gift cabinet especially designed. Most
exquisite octagonal pattern.
No. B3472

SALT AND PEPPER SET
(S. H. M. & Co.)
Bright finish. Height, 3½ inches.
Lined paper box. Cork aperture at
bottom. A lovely rounded octagonal
design.
No. B3463

SALT AND PEPPER SET
(S. H. M. & Co.)
Set contains three each salts and peppers,
height 1¾ inches, in richest gray silk case
made. Salts have gilt tops. Bright finish.
No. B3475

SALT AND PEPPER SET (S. H. M. & Co.)
Set contains six each salts and peppers. The salts have gilt
tops. Bright finish. Encased in the richest gray silk cabinet made.
Choice of two sizes, viz.: 1½ and 1¾ inches respectively.
No. B3476   Smaller size set.
No. B3477   Larger size set.

SALT OR PEPPER
(S. H. M. & Co.)
Bright finish. Salts have gilt
tops.
No. B3464   Salt,
No. B3465   Pepper,
(Cut actual size)

SALT OR PEPPER
(S. H. M. & Co.)
Bright finish. Salts have gilt
tops.
No. B3468   Salt,
No. B3469   Pepper,
Cut actual size)

TWELVE PIECE SALT SET (S. H. M. & Co.)
Set contains 6 open salts, diameter 1⅝ inches, hammered, gray finish and
six individual salt spoons. Encased in the richest gray silk presentation cabinet.
No. B3478

SALT AND PEPPER SET (S. H. M. & Co.)
Set contains three each salts and peppers in lined paper box.
The salts have gilt tops. Bright finish. Choice of two sizes, viz.: 1½
and 1¾ inches respectively.
No. B3473   Smaller size set,
No. B3474   Larger size set,

49

Solid Sterling Silver Table Service

GRAVY BOAT WITH TRAY (S. H. M. & Co.)
Solid Sterling Silver. Substantial weight. Elegantly constructed.
Bright finish.
No. B3392 Gravy Boat, length 6⅝ inches.
No. B3393 Tray, length 7¾ inches,

WATER PITCHER (S. H. M. & Co.)
Solid Sterling Silver very heavy weight. Capacity 4 pints. Height 9½ inches.
Bright finish. Possessing unquestionable dignity and character which is undeniable.
No. B3405

GRAVY BOAT WITH TRAY (S. H. M. & Co)
Solid Sterling silver. A popular style. Heavy weight. Bright finish.
No. B3396 Gravy Boat, length 8 inches.
No. B3397 Tray, length 8½ inches,

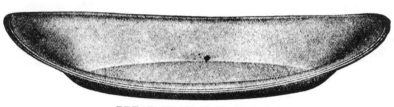

BREAD TRAY (S. H. M. & Co.)
Heavy threaded border. Bright finish. Length, 12½ inches.
No. B3414

BOWLS (S. H. M. & CO.)
The Lovely Persian pattern that is masterly
chased and finished in a rich Gray or Bright.
Choice of 8½ or 10-inch diameters. Heavy weight.
No. B3433 Diameter 8½ inches.
No. B3434. Diameter 10 inches.

BREAD TRAY (S. H. M. & Co)
Neatly pierced and richly embossed. Gray finish. Length,
10⅝ inches.
No. B3413 Each

GOBLET (S. H. M. & Co.)
Solid Sterling silver. Bright
finish. Height, 6 inches.
No. B3404

50

Solid Sterling Silver Sandwich or Cake Trays and Baskets

BOWL (S. H. M. & CO.)
Perfectly Plain in design. Very dignified and prepossessing. Bright Finish. Heavy weight. Diameter 8½ inches.
No. B3436

SANDWICH OR CAKE TRAY
(S. H. M. & Co.) 👉

Solid Sterling Silver. A most exquisite pattern, revealing mastership designing and unsurpassed construction and finish. Richly pierced and embossed. Choice of two sizes, 8½ or 10-inch diameters. Gray finish.

No.	Diameter
B3423	8½ inches.
B3424	10 inches.

Typical Profile of Sandwich Plates Nos. B3423, B3424.

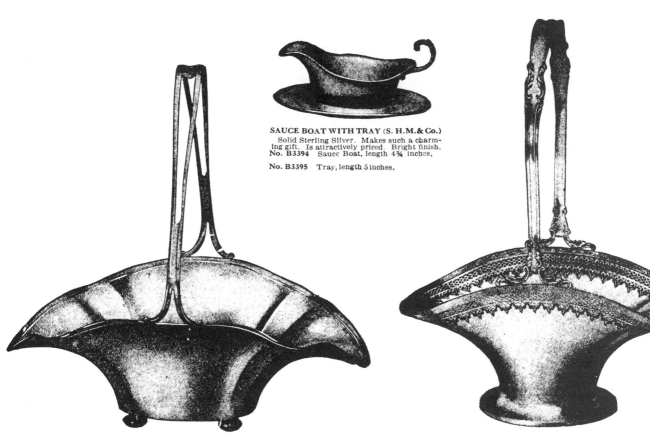

SAUCE BOAT WITH TRAY (S. H. M. & Co.)
Solid Sterling Silver. Makes such a charming gift. Is attractively priced. Bright finish.
No. B3394 Sauce Boat, length 4¾ inches.

No. B3395 Tray, length 5 inches.

FRUIT BASKET
Bright finish; fluted design; heavy weight. Height, including handle, 11½ inches.
No. B3437

FRUIT BASKET
Richly pierced and artistically embossed; gray finish. Height, including handle, 12¼ inches. Heavy weight.
No. B3438

Tomato Server and Berry Spoons
IN STERLING SILVER.

Berry Spoon.
No. 8266

Cucumber or Tomato Server.   Bright Handle, Gold-lined Bowl.
No. 8263 .

Colonial Gravy Ladle.   Gilt Bowl.
No. 8264 .

STERLING SILVER SUGAR SPOONS.

Illustrations Full Size.

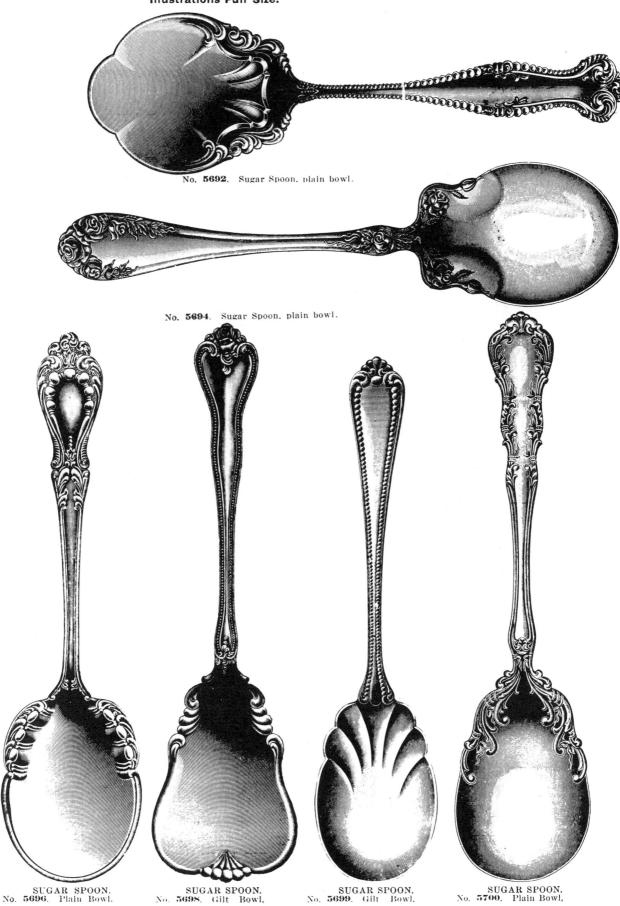

No. **5692**. Sugar Spoon, plain bowl.

No. **5694**. Sugar Spoon, plain bowl.

| SUGAR SPOON. | SUGAR SPOON. | SUGAR SPOON. | SUGAR SPOON. |
| No. **5696**. Plain Bowl. | No. **5698**. Gilt Bowl. | No. **5699**. Gilt Bowl. | No. **5700**. Plain Bowl. |

STERLING SILVER WARE.

Illustrations Actual Size.

No. **5715**. Pickle Fork, gold tines.

No. **5716**. Small Olive Fork, gold tines.

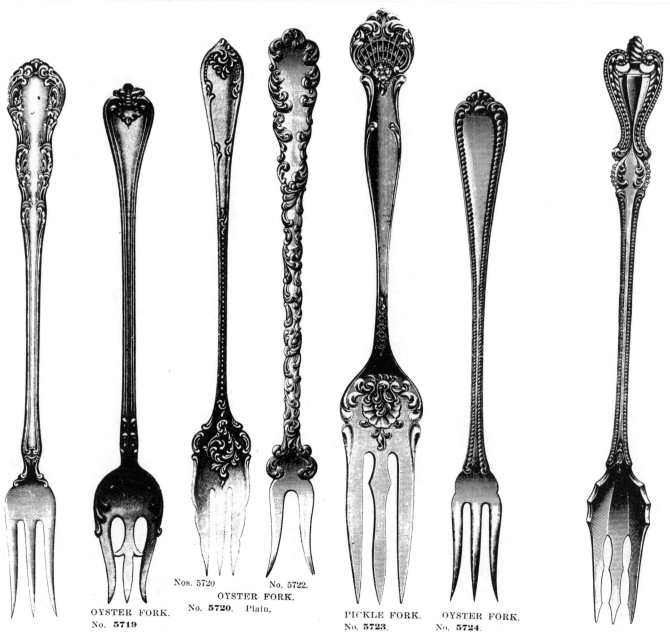

OYSTER FORK.
No. **5719**

Nos. 5720   No. 5722.
OYSTER FORK.
No. **5720**. Plain,

PICKLE FORK.
No. **5723**.

OYSTER FORK.
No. **5724**.

No. **5725**. Oyster Fork, plain

No. **5726**. Oyster Fork, plain tines.

STERLING SILVER WARE.

Showing Actual Size.

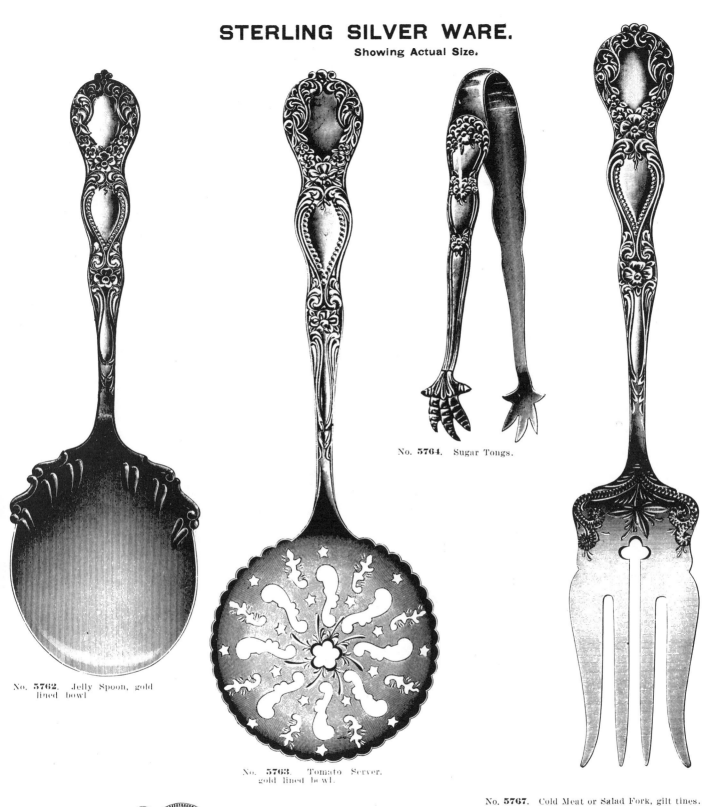

No. **5764**. Sugar Tongs.

No. **5762**. Jelly Spoon, gold lined bowl.

No. **5763**. Tomato Server, gold lined bowl.

No. **5767**. Cold Meat or Salad Fork, gilt tines.

No. **5766**. Cold Meat Fork, gilt tines.

Sterling Silver
Cream and Gravy
Ladles and

Cream Ladle. Bright Handle,
Gold-lined Bowl.
No. **8269**

Cream Ladle. Bright Handle and Bowl.
No. **8271**

Cream Ladle. Gilt Bowl and
French Grey Handle.
No. **8270**

Gravy Ladle. French Grey Handle,
Gold-lined Bowl.
No. **8272**

No. **5794**. Cream Ladle, gold bowl.

56

Sterling Silver Butter Knives and Spreaders.

Illustrations Full Size.

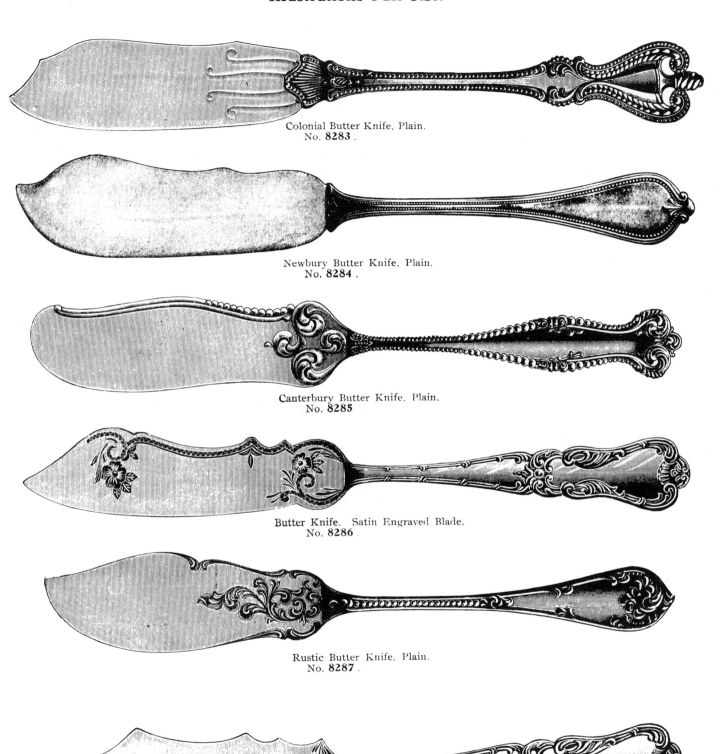

Colonial Butter Knife, Plain.
No. **8283** .

Newbury Butter Knife, Plain.
No. **8284** .

Canterbury Butter Knife, Plain.
No. **8285**

Butter Knife. Satin Engraved Blade.
No. **8286** .

Rustic Butter Knife, Plain.
No. **8287** .

Butter Knife. Satin Engraved Blade.
No. **8288** .

Sterling Silver Olive and Bon Bon Spoons.

Illustrations Full Size.

Olive Spoon, Pierced. Gold Lined Bowl, Bright Handle.
No. 8222.

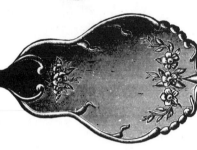

Olive Spoon. French Grey Finished Handle, Gold Lined Bowl.
No. 8223.

Pierced Olive Spoon. Spear End, Gold Lined Bowl.
No. 8224.

Bon Bon, Pierced. Gold Lined Bowl, French Grey Handle.
No. 8225.

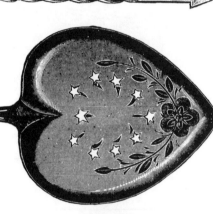

Bon Bon, Pierced. Gold Lined Bowl, Bright Handle.
No. 8226.

Bon Bon, Pierced. Gold Lined Bowl, Bright Handle.
No. 8227.

Sugar Sifter. Bright Finish, Gold Lined Bowl.
No. 8228.

Bon Bon, Pierced. Gold Lined Bowl, French
Grey Handle.
No. 8230.

STERLING SILVER TEA STRAINERS, TEA BALL

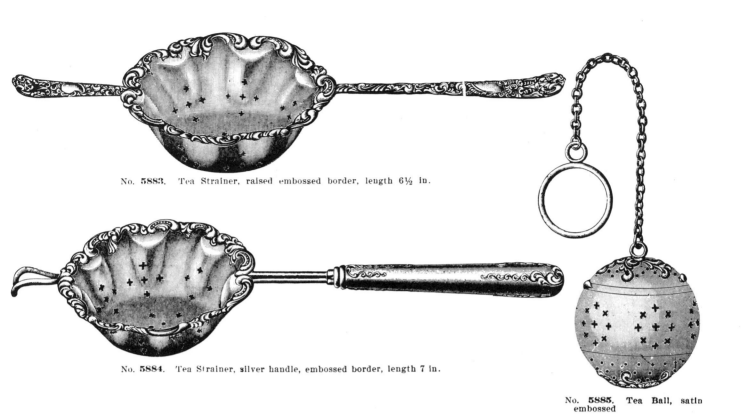

No. **5883.** Tea Strainer, raised embossed border, length 6½ in.

No. **5884.** Tea Strainer, silver handle, embossed border, length 7 in.

No. **5885.** Tea Ball, satin embossed

No. **5889.** Tea Strainer, ebony handle, raised b o r d e r length 6¾ inches.

No. **5887.** Tea Strainer, gold lined, shown actual size.

TEA BALL (WATROUS)
Bright; cut actual size.
No. T3339

TEA BALL (WATROUS)
Bright; cut actual size.
No. T3336

Solid Sterling Silver Articles

VASES

A beautiful octagonal design which is obtainable in a masterly engraved pattern as shown or perfectly plain if desired. Base weighted and reinforced with cement. Choice of four sizes:

Plain Design

No.	
1E220A	8-inch
1E220B	10-inch
1E220C	12-inch
1E220D	14-inch

Engraved Design

No.	
1E220E	8-inch
1E220F	10-inch
1E220G	12-inch
1E220H	14-inch

VASES

A magnificent closely fluted pattern, with choice of an artistically engraved design as shown or perfectly plain as quoted. Base weighted and reinforced with cement. Choice of four sizes:

Plain Design

No.	
1E222A	8-inch
1E222B	10-inch
1E222C	12-inch
1E222D	14-inch

Engraved Design

No.	
1E222E	8-inch
1E222F	10-inch
1E222G	12-inch
1E222H.	14-inch

VASES

Designed octagonally with alternate richly engraved and plain panels or all perfectly plain as quoted. Base weighted and reinforced with cement. Choice of four sizes:

Plain Design

No.	
1E225A	8-inch
1E225B	10-inch
1E225C	12-inch
1E225D	14-inch

Engraved Design

No.	
1E225E	8-inch
1E225F	10-inch
1E225G	12-inch
1E225H	14-inch

VASES

A loving cup style vase that has always proven popular. You have the choice of an artistic design in engraving which is masterly executed or a perfectly plain so keeping with a dignified atmosphere. Base is weighted and reinforced with cement. Choice of three sizes as quoted:

Plain Design

No.	
1E605A	9-inch
1E605B	11-inch
1E605C	13-inch

Engraved Design

No.	
1E605D	9-inch
1E605E	11-inch
1E605F	13-inch

VASES

A design that is very prepossessing in appearance. Square with rounded corners giving it the desired semi-octagonal shape. Choice of engraved design as illustrated or perfectly plain. Base is weighted and reinforced with cement. Made in three fast selling sizes:

Plain Design

No.	
1E250A	10-inch
1E250B	12-inch
1E250C	14-inch

Engraved Design

No.	
1E250D	10-inch
1E250E	12-inch
1E250F	14-inch

Sterling Silver Candlesticks

CANDLESTICKS

A beautiful semi-octagonal design, richly fluted. Weighted and reinforced with cement. Choice of a perfectly plain or artistically engraved design as shown. Made in four sizes:

Plain Design.

No.	
1E161A	8-inch
1E161B	10-inch
1E161C	12-inch
1E161D	14-inch

Engraved Design

No.	
1E161E	8-inch
1E161F	10-inch
1E161G	12-inch
1E161H	14-inch

CANDLESTICKS

A semi-octagonal design with pronounced fluting. Choice of a perfectly plain or magnificently engraved design as shown. Weighted and reinforced with cement. Made in four sizes:

Plain Design

No.	
1E121A	8-inch
1E121B	10-inch
1E121C	12-inch
1E121D	14-inch

Engraved Design

No.	
1E121E	8-inch
1E121F	10-inch
1E121G	12-inch
1E121H	14-inch

CANDLESTICKS

A square design with rounded fluted corners. Choice of a perfectly plain or richly engraved design as shown. Weighted and reinforced with cement. Made in four sizes:

Plain Design

No.	
1E160A	8-inch
1E160B	10-inch
1E160C	12-inch
1E160D	14-inch

Engraved Design

No.	
1E160E	8-inch
1E160F	10-inch
1E160G	12-inch
1E160H	14-inch

CANDLESTICKS

A symmetrical octagonal design with choice of a perfectly plain or artistically engraved pattern, in which base is engraved as well. Weighted and reinforced with cement. Choice of four sizes:

Plain Design

No.	
1E120A	8-inch
1E120B	10-inch
1E120C	12-inch
1E120D	14-inch

Engraved Design

No.	
1E120E	8-inch
1E120F	10-inch
1E120G	12-inch
1E120H	14-inch

CANDLESTICKS

A nicely tapered candlestick, designed square with bulging rounded corners, nicely fluted. It is masterly engraved on all four sides as well as the base. Also furnished perfectly plain as quoted. Weighted and reinforced with cement. Choice of two most popular selling sizes:

Plain Design

No	
1E140A	10-inch
1E140B	12-inch

Engraved Design

No	
1E140C	10-inch
1E140D	12-inch

STERLING SILVER CUPS, BON BONS, ETC., GUARANTEED $\frac{925}{1000}$ FINE.

No. C1452 Sugar bowl.

No. C1452   Cream Pitcher

No. C1019   Bon Bon.
Diameter, 6 inches.

No. C1016 Bon Bon
Diameter, 5 inches.

No. C1104   Cup En-
graved Gilt.
Plain gilt.

No. C1014   Bon Bon.
Diameter, 4¾ inches.

No. C1109 Cup gilt

No. C1115 Cup, gilt.

No. C73   Tea Bell

No. C215   Flask

No. C71   Tea Bell.

Prices Each.

No. C180   Puff Box _____

No. C181   Puff Box _____

C20   Tea Caddy_____

No. C301   Salt _____

No. C435   Salve Box __

No. C511   Puff Box __

No. C27   Tea Strainer _____

No. C1921   Tea Strainer_____

No. C301   Pep-
per_____

No. C1641 Sugar
Sifter____

No C225 Pin tray.

No C227 Pin Tray,
Length, 4½ inches.

No. C228   Pin Tray _____

No. C1791   **Tray** _____

No. **6448.** Prize Cup, burnished, engraved.

No. **6449.** Prize Cup, G. L., 3 handles, height 9 in.

No. **6450.** Loving Cup, 3 handles, burnished, gold lined, height 4 in.

No. **6451.** Loving Cup, burnished beaded, gold lined, height 3¾ in.
No. **6452.** Loving Cup, burnished, beaded, gold lined, height 4¾ in.
No. **6453.** Loving Cup, burnished, beaded. gold lined, height 6¼ in.

No. **6454.** Loving Cup, height 5½ in.

STERLING SILVER TEA SETS, ETC.

Gauranteed 925-1000 Fine.

No. C1553 Sugar Bowl....
Height, 3½ inches.

No. C1553 Cream Pitcher....
Height, 3 inches.

No. C. 1555 Coffee Pot. Height, 9 inches.....

No. C1553 Tea pot. Height, 5 inches....

No. C1980 Tray. Length, 10½ inches......

No. C. 1555 Tea Pot. Height, 6 inches.......

No. C1555 Sugar Bowl. Height, 5 inches.....

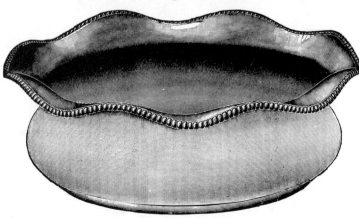

No. C1452 Berry Bowl. Diameter, 7¼ inches.....

No. C1555 Cream Pitcher, Gilt. Height, 4 in...
Spoon Holder to match. Height, 3¾ in........

STERLING TABLE WARE.
Wentworth Pattern.

Butter Knife, plain blade
Gilt blade.

Cold Meat Fork, plain tines.
"   "   gilt "

Sugar Spoon, plain bowl
Gilt bowl

Fish Fork, plain tines
Gilt tines

Coffee Spoon,
plain bowls
gilt "

Fish Knife, plain blade
Gilt blade

Fancy Pieces Put Up in White Enameled Silk Lined Boxes.

STERLING TABLE WARE $\frac{925}{1000}$ FINE.
Wentworth Pattern.

Ice Cream Server, plain blade
Gilt blade

Soup Ladle, plain bowl
Gilt bowl

Gravy Ladle, plain bowl
Gilt bowl

Cream Ladle, plain bowl
Gilt bowl

Sugar Tongs

Ice Cream Spoon, plain bowl
Gilt bowl

Fancy pieces in white enameled silk lined boxes.

Small Berry or Salad Spoon, plain bowl.
" " " " gilt bowl

Pickle Fork, plain tines.
" " gilt tines

Salad Fork, plain tines
" " gilt tines

Oyster Fork, plain tines
" " gilt tines.

Large Berry Spoon, plain bowl.
" " gilt bowl

Fancy pieces come in white enameled silk lined boxes.

STERLING TABLE WARE $\frac{925}{1000}$ FINE

Tudor Pattern.

Small Berry or Salad spoon, plain bowl
" " " " gilt

Pickle Fork, plain tines
" " gilt

Salad Fork, plain tines
" " gilt

Oyster Fork, plain tines
" " gilt

Nut or Ice Spoon, gilt bowl
" " plain "

Fancy pieces in white enameled, silk lined boxes.

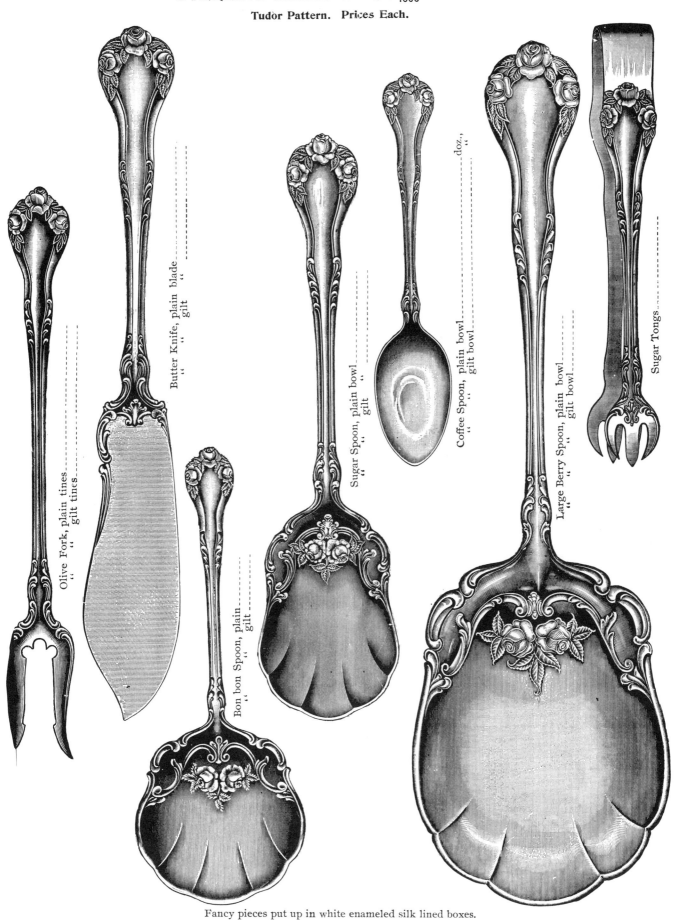

Olive Fork, plain tines
"   "   gilt tines

Butter Knife, plain blade
"   "   gilt

Bon bon Spoon, plain
"   "   gilt

Sugar Spoon, plain bowl
"   "   gilt

Coffee Spoon, plain bowl
"   "   gilt bowl
doz.,

Large Berry Spoon, plain bowl
"   "   gilt bowl

Sugar Tongs

Fancy pieces put up in white enameled silk lined boxes.

Sugar Sifter, plain bowl
" " gilt "

Cold Meat Fork
plain tines
" gilt "

Cream Ladle, plain bowl
" " gilt "

Gravy Ladle, plain bowl
" " gilt "

Soup Ladle, plain bowl
" " gilt "

Olive Spoon, plain bowl
" " gilt "

STERLING TABLE WARE $\frac{925}{1000}$ FINE.

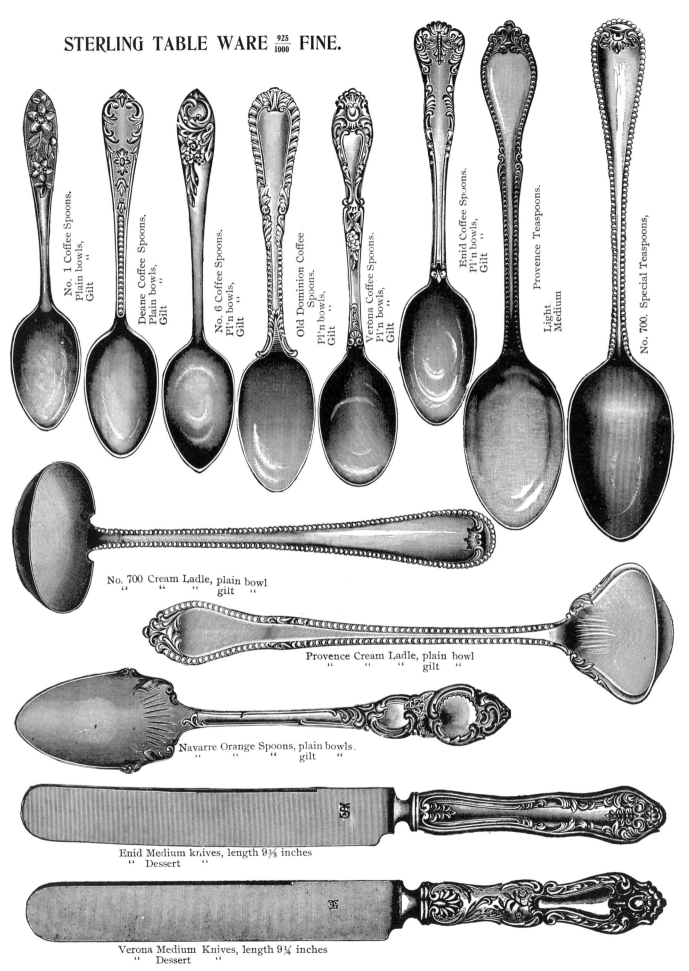

No. 1 Coffee Spoons.
Plain bowls,
" Gilt

Deane Coffee Spoons.
Plain bowls,
" Gilt "

No. 6 Coffee Spoons.
Pl'n bowls,
" Gilt "

Old Dominion Coffee
Spoons.
Pl'n bowls,
" Gilt "

Verona Coffee Spoons.
Pl'n bowls,
" Gilt "

Enid Coffee Spoons.
Pl'n bowls,
" Gilt "

Provence Teaspoons.
Light
Medium

No. 700. Special Teaspoons,

No. 700 Cream Ladle, plain bowl
" " " gilt "

Provence Cream Ladle, plain bowl
" " " gilt "

Navarre Orange Spoons, plain bowls
" " " gilt "

Enid Medium knives, length 9⅜ inches
" Dessert "

Verona Medium Knives, length 9¼ inches
" Dessert "

71

Provenee Butter Knife, plain blade......
Gilt blade----------------------------

Old Colony Butter Knife, plain blade...
Gilt blade ---------------------

Verona Butter Knife, plain blade....
Gilt blade----------------------
Engraved gilt blade ------------

No. 700 Butter Knife, plain blade....
Gilt blade ----------------------

Provence Sugar Spoon, plain bowl......
Gilt bowl----------------------------

Old Colony Sugar Spoon, plain bowl-------------------
Gilt bowl ----------------------------------

Verona Sugar Spoon,
Plain bowl------------
Gilt bowl------------
Engraved gilt bowl----

Old Dominion Sugar Spoon,
Plain bowl--------------------
Gilt bowl --------------------

No. 800   Cream Ladle, gilt bowl only.

No. 800   Sugar Sifter, gilt bowl only.

No. 800   Cold Meat or Beef Fork, engraved, gilt only.

No. 800   Tomato Server, gold bowl only -

No. 800 Sugar Spoon, gold bowl only.

No. 800   Jelly Server, gold bowl only

No. 800   Olive Spoon, gilt bowl only

No. 800   Sardine Fork, gilt tines only

No. 800   Berry Spoon, gilt bowl only

STERLING SILVER $\frac{925}{1000}$ FINE.

Warwick Small Meat Fork, Plain ....
"   "   "   "   gilt ....

Warwick Large Meat Fork, plain ....
"   "   "   "   gilt ....

Warwick Pickle Fork, plain ....
"   "   "   gilt ....

Warwick Picallili Spoon, plain ....
"   "   "   gilt ....

Warwick Small Cheese Scoop, plain ....
"   "   "   "   gilt ....

Warwick Sugar Shell, plain ....
"   "   "   gilt ....

Warwick Butter Knife, plain ....
"   "   "   gilt ....

All fancy pieces in paper silk lined boxes.

74

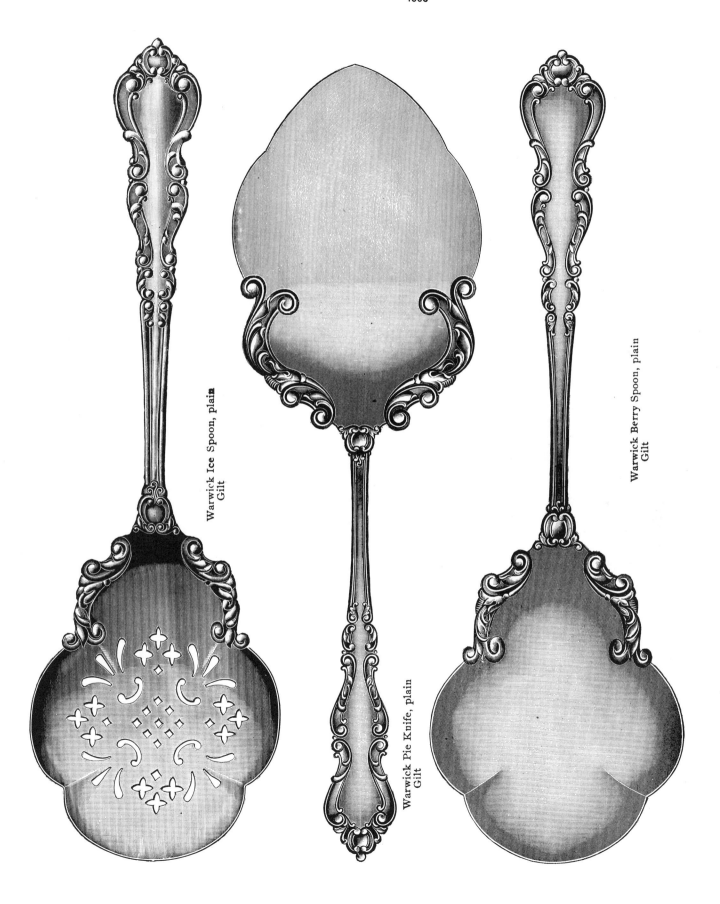

Warwick Ice Spoon, plain
Gilt

Warwick Pie Knife, plain
Gilt

Warwick Berry Spoon, plain
Gilt

STERLING SILVER, $\frac{925}{1000}$ FINE.

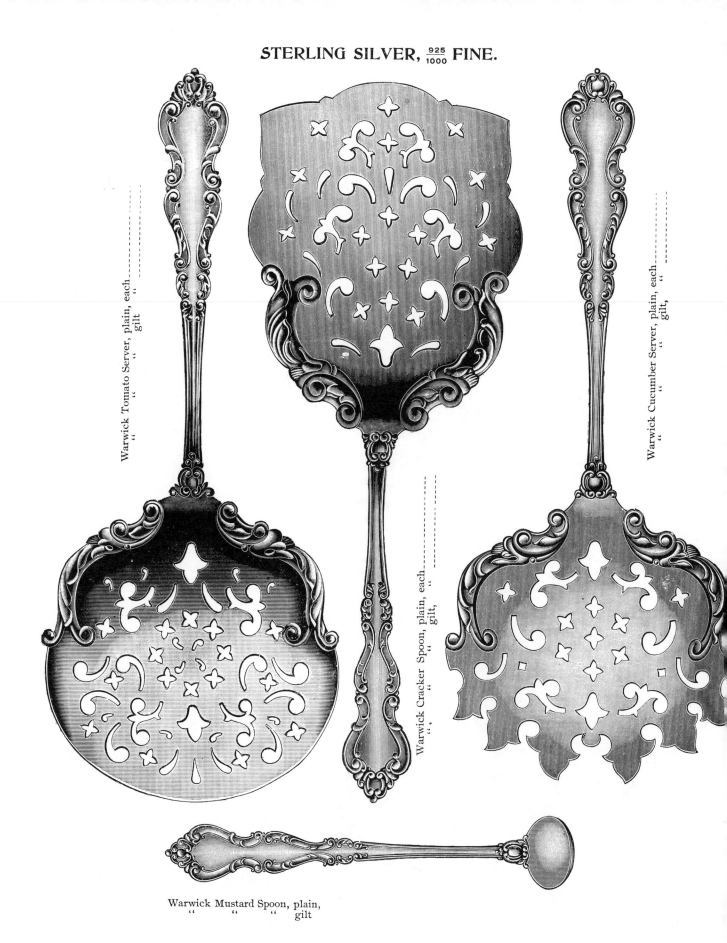

Warwick Tomato Server, plain, each
" " gilt

Warwick Cracker Spoon, plain, each
" " gilt,

Warwick Cucumber Server, plain, each
" " gilt,

Warwick Mustard Spoon, plain,
" " " gilt

All Fancy Pieces in Paper Silk Lined Boxes.

76

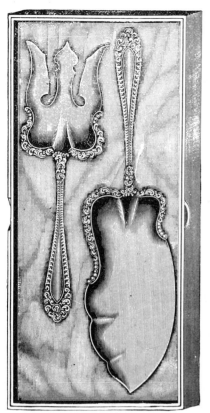

Kenilworth Fish Set.
Plain, each ....
Gilt, each ....

Kenilworth Berry Spoon.
Plain bowl, each ....
Gilt bowl, each ....

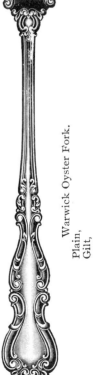

Kenilworth Salad Set.
Plain, each
Gilt, each

Warwick Small Cream Ladle.
Plain, each ....
Gilt, each ....

Warwick Ice Cream Spoons.
Plain,
Gilt,

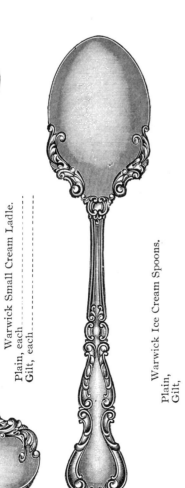

Warwick Orange Spoon
Plain,
Gilt,

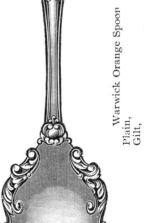

Warwick Oyster Fork.
Plain,
Gilt,

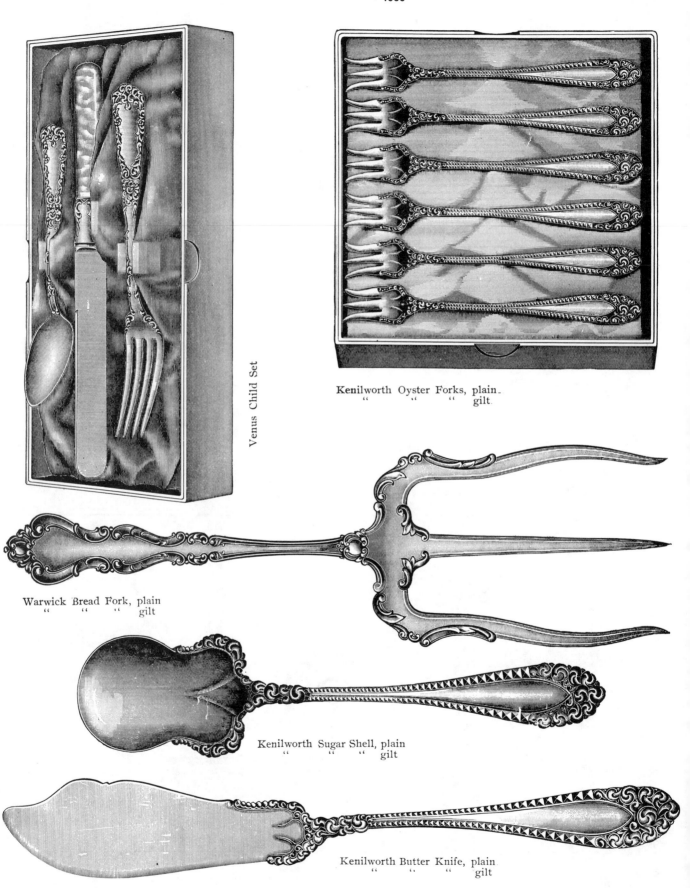

Venus Child Set

Kenilworth Oyster Forks, plain
"   "   "   gilt

Warwick Bread Fork, plain
"   "   "   gilt

Kenilworth Sugar Shell, plain
"   "   "   gilt

Kenilworth Butter Knife, plain
"   "   "   gilt

All fancy pieces in paper silk lined boxes.

STERLING SILVER SPOONS AND FORKS, $\frac{925}{1000}$ FINE.

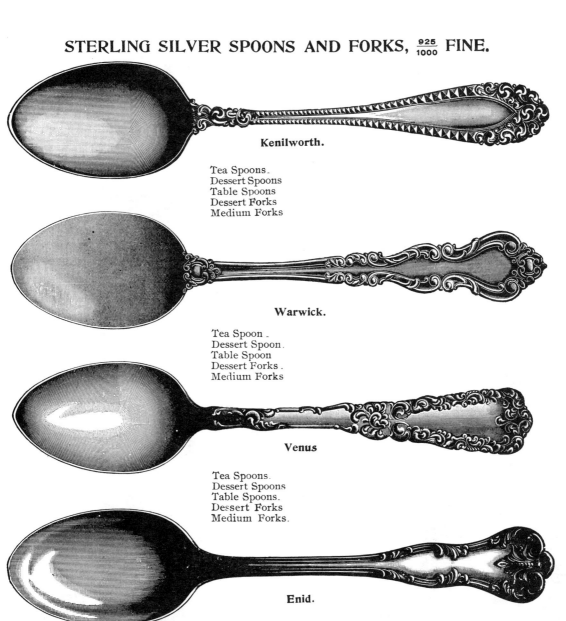

Kenilworth.

Tea Spoons.
Dessert Spoons
Table Spoons
Dessert Forks
Medium Forks

Warwick.

Tea Spoon.
Dessert Spoon.
Table Spoon
Dessert Forks.
Medium Forks

Venus

Tea Spoons.
Dessert Spoons
Table Spoons.
Dessert Forks
Medium Forks.

Enid.

Tea spoons
Dessert Spoons
Table Spoons.
Dessert Forks.
Medium Forks

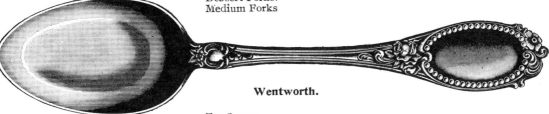

Wentworth.

Tea Spoons
Dessert Spoons.
Table Spoons
Dessert Forks
Medium Forks

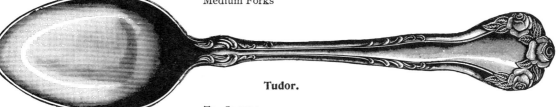

Tudor.

Tea Spoons
Dessert Spoons
Table Spoons
Dessert Forks
Medium Forks

STERLING SILVER $\frac{925}{1000}$ FINE.

Venus Cream Ladle, gilt bowl

Venus Sugar Sifter, gilt

Venus Berry Set, plain
Gilt

Venns Sugar Shell, plain No. 1 bowl
Gilt No. 1 bowl

Warwick Sugar Tong, large.

Venus Sardine Fork, gilt.

Venus Coffee Spoons, plain. , gilt,
All fancy pieces in paper silk lined boxes.

80

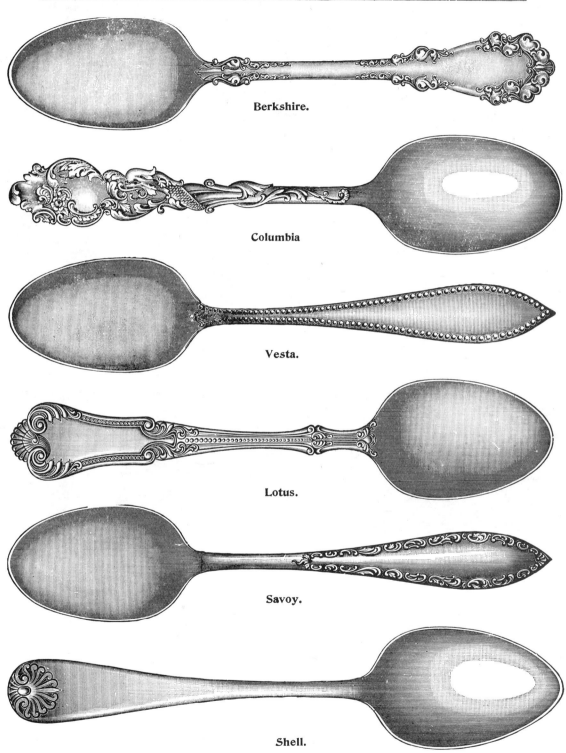

SPOONS, FORKS, ETC. STAMPED
·1847· ROGERS BROS.
ARE GENUINE „ROGERS" GOODS.

Berkshire.

Columbia

Vesta.

Lotus.

Savoy.

Shell.

TIPPED AND SHELL PATTERNS.	Extra Plate. A1	Sec'nl Plate. X 11	Triple Plate. No. 6
Tea Spoons			
Table Spoons			
Desert Spoons			
Medium Forks			
Desert Forks			

FANCY PATTERNS.	Extra Plate. A1	Sec'nl Plate. X 11	Triple Plate. No. 6
Tea Spoons			
Table Spoons			
Desert Spoons			
Medium Forks			
Desert Forks			

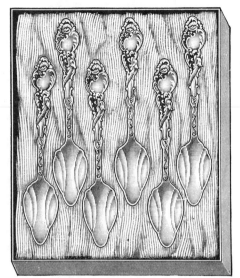

No. 681 Savoy Long Pickle Fork in lined box,

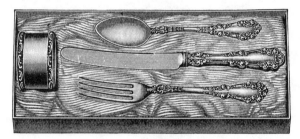

No. 647 Columbia Orange Spoons,
Gilt bowls.

No. 703 Berkshire Child's Set in lined box.

No. 604 Portland
Butter Knife and
Sugar Shell in
box, per set.

No. 615 Berkshire Berry Spoon in lined box.
    "   "   "   gilt bowl in lined box.

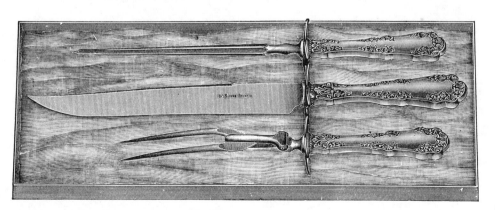

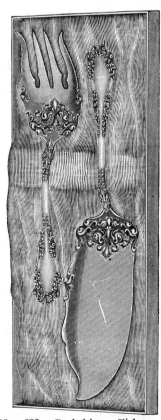

No. 657 Berkshire Carving Set, three pieces, nickel silver, silver soldered, hollow handle, in lined box.

No. 638 Berkshire Fish
Knife and Fork, in box,

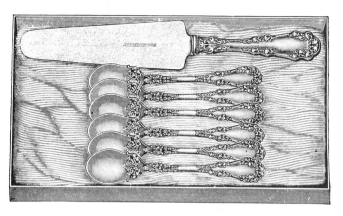

SPOONS, FORKS, ETC. STAMPED
·1847· ROGERS BROS.
ARE GENUINE „ROGERS" GOODS.

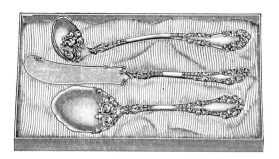

No. 702 Berkshire
One each Cream Ladle, Twist Butter Knife and Sugar Shell.
Lotus, Vesta, Columbia and Savoy same price.

No. 708 Berkshire
One Pie or Ice Cream Server and Six Ice Cream Spoons.

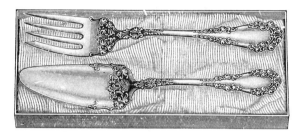

No. 701 Berkshire
One each, Jelly Knife and Cold Meat Fork, large.

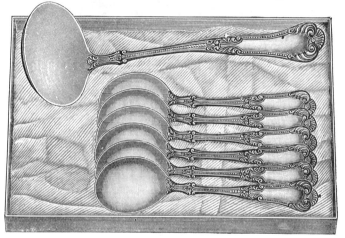

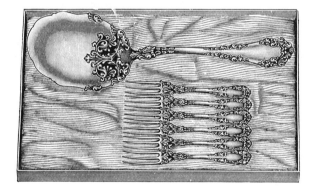

No. 709 Lotus
One Oyster Ladle and six Soup Spoons.

No. 706 Berkshire
One Berry Spoon and six Berry Forks.
Portland, Lotus, Columbia and Savoy.

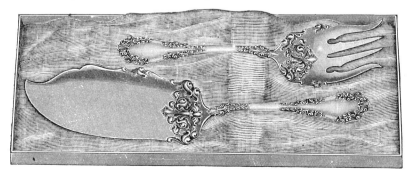

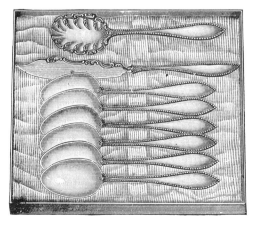

No. 638 Berkshire
Fish Knife and Fork.

No. 710 Vesta
One each, Butter Knife and Sugar Shell and six
Teaspoons. Berkshire, Lotus, Columbia, Savoy
and Portland same price.

83

Newton

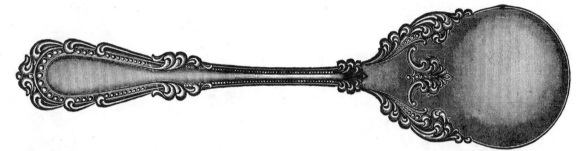

Milton.

Newton.

Plato.

Milton.

Fancy Sugar Shells, extra plate _____
   "   "   "   triple plate _____
Gilt bowls, extra _____
Put up one each in fancy lined box, extra _____
Fancy Twist Handle Butter Knife, extra plate _____
   "   "   "   "   "   triple plate _____
Gilt blades, extra _____
Put up one each in fancy lined box, extra _____

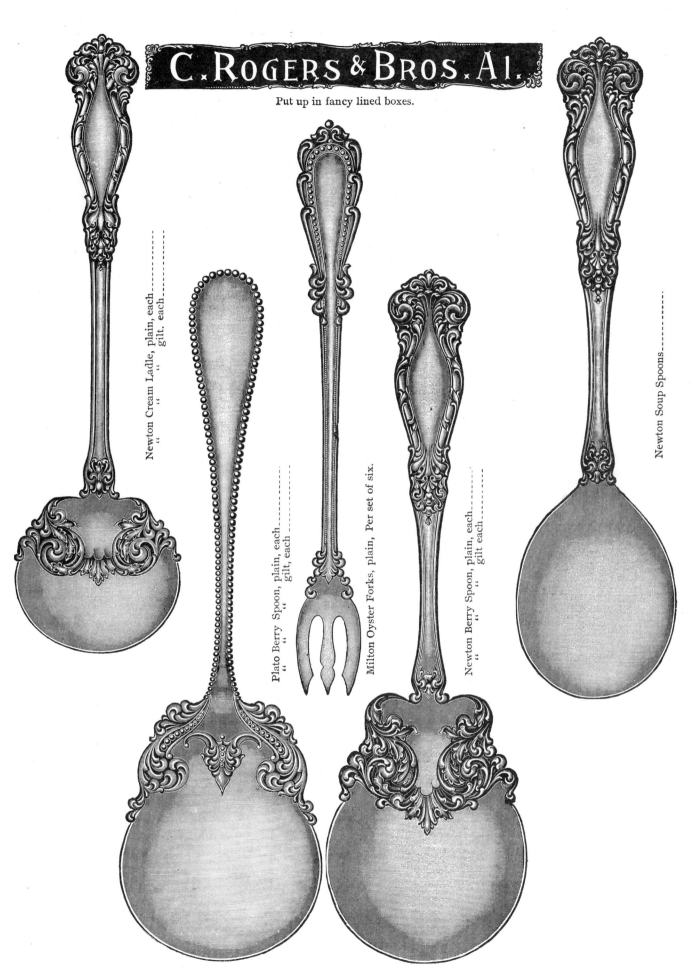

Put up in fancy lined boxes.

Newton Cream Ladle, plain, each
" " gilt. each

Plato Berry Spoon, plain, each
" " gilt, each

Milton Oyster Forks, plain, Per set of six.

Newton Berry Spoon, plain, each
" " gilt each

Newton Soup Spoons

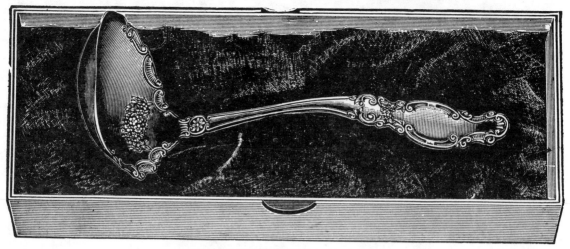

MELROSE OYSTER LADLE (reduced size.)

Melrose Cream Ladle	Gold bowl	Bright cut and gold bowl
" Gravy Ladle	Gold bowl	Bright cut and gold bowl
" Oyster Ladle	Gold bowl	Bright cut and gold bowl
" medium sized Soup Ladle	Gold bowl	
" large Soup Ladle	Gold bowl	

Also furnished in Blenheim, Seville and Yale pattern.   Each in fancy lined box.

Melrose Cold Meat Fork (small size).   Gold tines
Also furnished in Yale, Seville and Blenheim pattern.   Each in fancy lined box.

Seville Berry or Fruit Forks   Gold tines extra
Also furnished in Melrose, Yale and Blenheim pattern.   Packed ½ dozen in fancy lined box.

Yale Individual Salad Forks   Gold tines extra
Also furnished in Melrose pattern.   Packed ½ dozen in fancy lined box.

Melrose Pickle Fork   Fancy lined box to hold one, extra
Also furnished in Yale pattern.

Melroae Individual Fish Forks   Gold tines, extra
Also furnished in Yale pattern.   Packed ½ dozen in fancy lined box.

Melrose Berry Spoon
Plain bowl _____
Gilt   "   _____
  "   "   bright cut _____

Yale Berry Spoon.
Plain bowl _____
Gilt   "   _____
  "   "   bright cut _____
All Fancy Pieces come in silk lined case.

Blenheim Berry Spoon.
Plain bowl _____
Gilt   "   _____
  "   "   bright cut _____

87

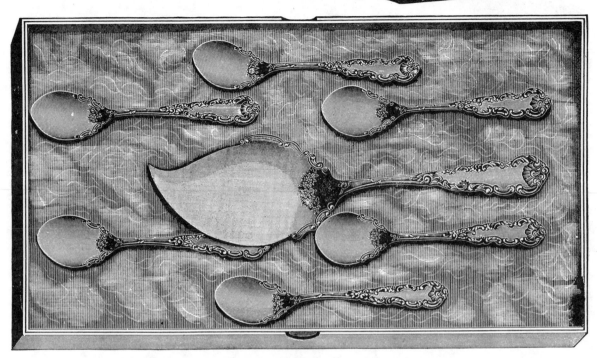

No. 154   Cordova Ice Cream Set.   Ice Cream Knife and one-half dozen Ice Cream Spoons.

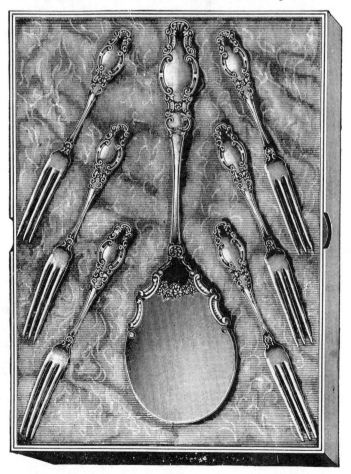

Yale Pie Server. (Hollow handle).

No. 155   Melrose Berry Set.   One Berry Spoon and one-half dozen Three Tined Berry Forks.

Yale Sugar Shell and Twist Butter Knife, in white lined box. Per pair, plain, Gilt sugar and butter Engraved and gold Furnished in all fancy patterns.

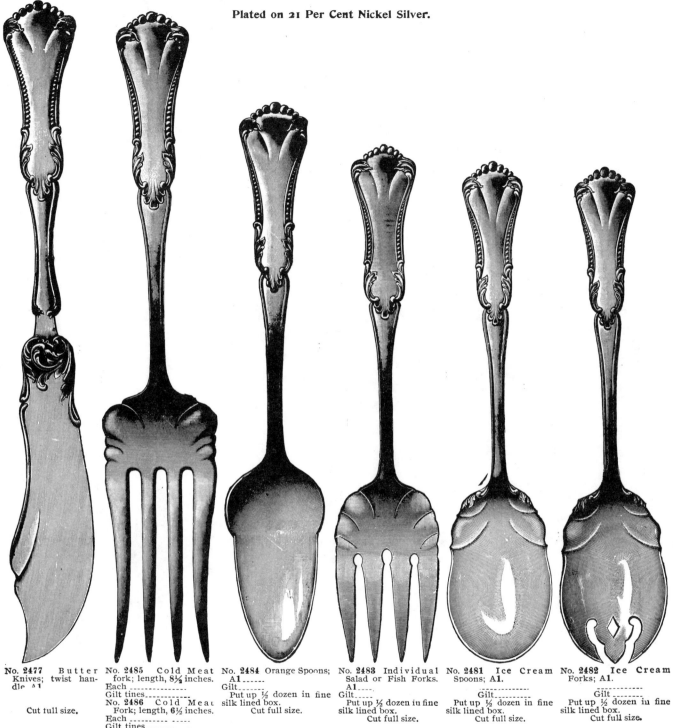

No. 2477   Butter Knives; twist handle A1

Cut full size.

No. 2485   Cold Meat fork; length, 8½ inches.
Each _____
Gilt tines_____
No. 2486   Cold Meat Fork; length, 6½ inches.
Each _____
Gilt tines_____
Put up in fine silk lined box.

No. 2484 Orange Spoons; A1 _____
Gilt_____
Put up ½ dozen in fine silk lined box.
Cut full size.

No. 2483 Individual Salad or Fish Forks. A1____
Gilt____
Put up ½ dozen in fine silk lined box.
Cut full size.

No. 2481   Ice Cream Spoons; A1.
_____
Gilt_____
Put up ½ dozen in fine silk lined box.
Cut full size.

No. 2482   Ice Cream Forks; A1.
_____
Gilt _____
Put up ½ dozen in fine silk lined box.
Cut full size.

The Marcella Pattern.

No. 2478 Sugar Shells; A1 _____
No. 2480 Butter Knife and Sugar Shell; A1.   Put up in fine silk lined box
No. 2479 Sugar Shells; with gold bowls_____
Cut full size.

Melrose Child Set, extra plate, three pieces in silk lined box.
Furnished in all patterns. Per doz. sets _____

Melrose Ice Cream Spoons, also furnished in Yale pattern.
Packed ½ doz. in fancy lined box._____
Gold bowls, extra_____

Melrose Orange Spoons, also furnished in Yale and Seville
pattern. Packed ½ doz. in fancy lined box.__
Gold bowls_____

Yale Cold Tea Spoons..A1
Triple_____

Melrose Bouillon Spoons, also furnished in Yale pattern.
Packed ½ doz. in fancy lined box. Extra plate____
Triple plate_____
Gold bowls, extra _____

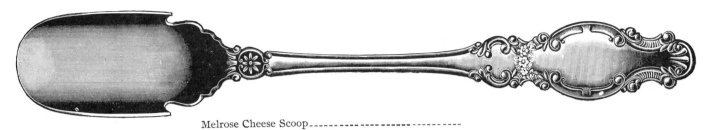

Melrose Cheese Scoop------------------------------------

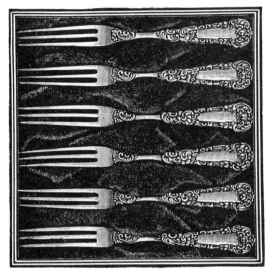

Yale Berry Forks, 2 tines, Plain------
"   "   "   "   Gilt--------

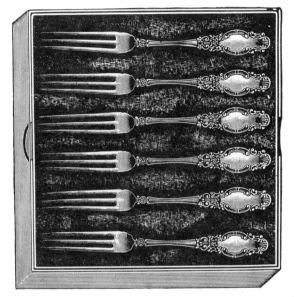

Melrose Berry Forks, 3 tines, Plain----
"   "   "   "   Gilt------

Yale Orange Spoons.   Plain------------------
"   "   "   Gilt--------------------

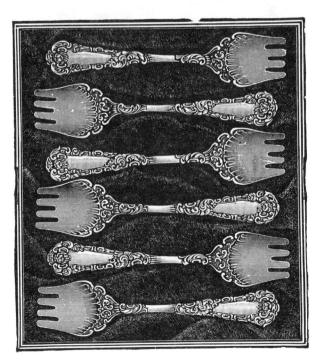

Yale Ice Cream Forks,   Plain------------------
"   "   "   Gilt--------------------

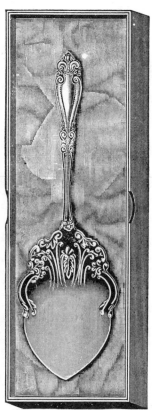

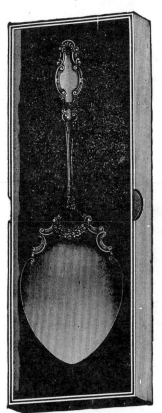

Yale Crumb Knife.

Plain, each _ _ _ _ _ _ _ _ _ _ _
Gilt, " _ _ _ _ _ _ _ _ _ _ _

Blenheim Pie Knife.

Plain _ _ _ _ _ _ _ _ _ _ _ _ _
Gilt _ _ _ _ _ _ _ _ _ _ _ _ _
Bright Cut Gilt _ _ _ _ _

Melrose Pie Knife.

Plain _ _ _ _ _ _ _ _ _ _ _ _ _
Gilt _ _ _ _ _ _ _ _ _ _ _ _ _
Bright Cut _ _ _ _ _ _ _ _

Yale Salad Set.

Plain _ _ _ _ _ _ _ _ _ _ _ _ _
Gilt _ _ _ _ _ _ _ _ _ _ _ _ _

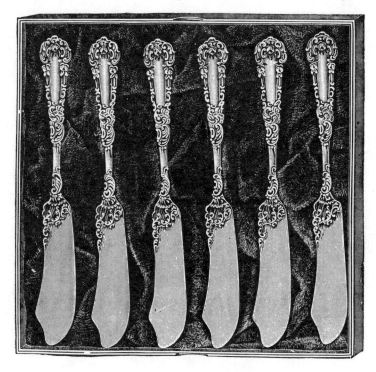

Yale Individual Butter Spreaders.

Also furnished in Melrose and Blenheim.

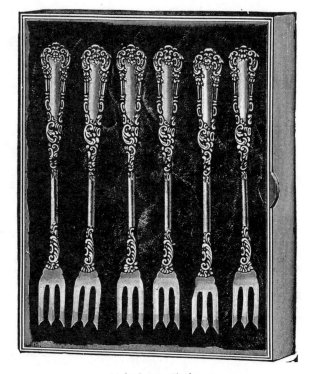

Yale Oyster Forks.

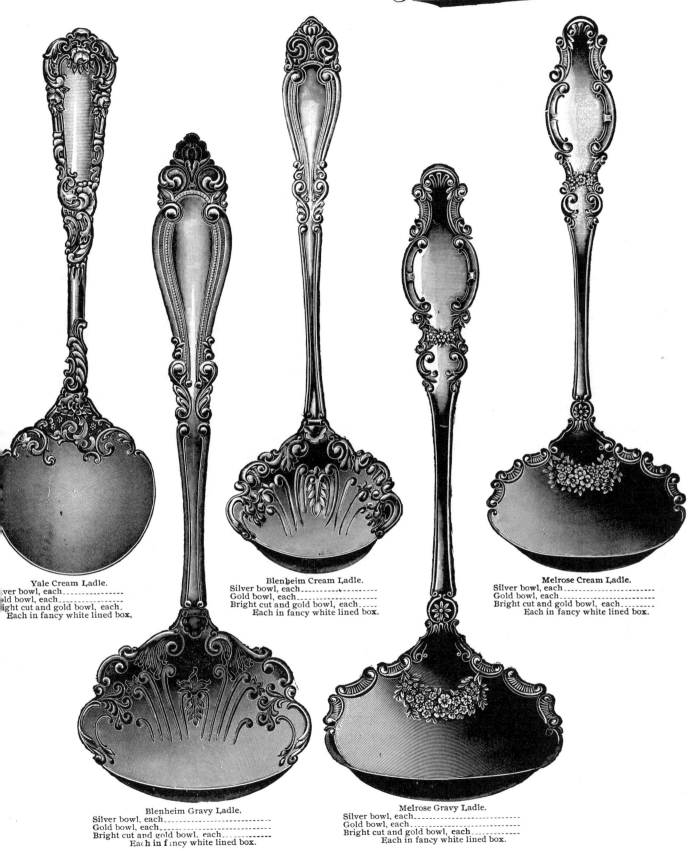

❦W✶ROGERS;★ "Eagle Brand"
Wallingford, Ct.

Yale Cream Ladle.
ver bowl, each
ld bowl, each
ight cut and gold bowl, each
Each in fancy white lined box,

Blenheim Cream Ladle.
Silver bowl, each
Gold bowl, each
Bright cut and gold bowl, each
Each in fancy white lined box.

Melrose Cream Ladle.
Silver bowl, each
Gold bowl, each
Bright cut and gold bowl, each
Each in fancy white lined box.

Blenheim Gravy Ladle.
Silver bowl, each
Gold bowl, each
Bright cut and gold bowl, each
Each in fancy white lined box.

Melrose Gravy Ladle.
Silver bowl, each
Gold bowl, each
Bright cut and gold bowl, each
Each in fancy white lined box.

All fancy pieces put up in fancy box.

No. **7760** Medium Knives, plain or satin handles   No. **7760** Dessert Knives, plain or satin handles.

No. **7770** Medium Forks, plain or satin handles.   No. **7770** Dessert Forks, plain or satin handles.

No. **8760** Medium Knives or Forks, plain or satin handles.   No. **8760** Dessert Knives or Forks, plain or satin handles.

No. **7730** Medium Knives or Forks

No. **7720** Medium Knives or Forks.   No. **7720** Dessert Knives or Forks..

No. **7790** Medium Knives or Forks, plain or satin handles..   No. **7790** Dessert Knives or Forks, plain or satin handles.

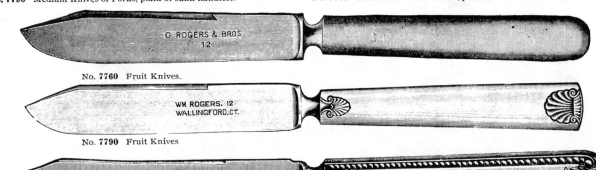

No. **7760** Fruit Knives.

No. **7790** Fruit Knives

No. **7720** Fruit Knives

C. ROGERS & BROS. A1.

Square.

Nickel Silver Medium Forks..   Satin Handle......   Nickel Silver Dessert Forks.

Square.

Steel Medium Knives   Satin Handle   Steel Dessert Knives.

Windsor.

Steel Medium Knives..   Steel Desert Knives..
Nickel Silver Medium Forks.   Nickel Silver Dessert Forks

Shell.

Steel Medium Knives..   Steel Dessert Knives..
Nickel Silver Medium Forks.   Nickel Silver Dessert Forks.

Embossed.

Steel Medium Knives.......   Steel Dessert Knives---------------------
Nickel Silver Medium Forks..   Nickel Silver Dessert Forks ---------------

Milton Hollow Handle.

Steel Medium Knives -------------------   Steel Dessert Knives-------------------
Nickel Silver Medium Forks -------------   Nickel Silver Dessert Forks ----------------

Put up in fancy lined boxes.

Regent Berry Fork

Newton Child's Set

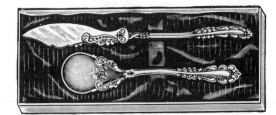

Milton Sugar Shell and Butter Knife Set
"   "   "   "   "   "   " gold shell

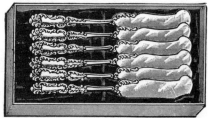

Regent Individual Butter Knives................Set of six,

Regent Coffee Set complete
"   "   "   " with gold spoons.

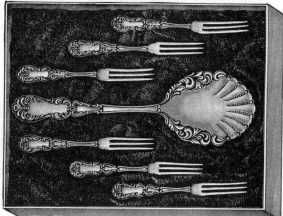

Regent Berry Set
"   "   " gold spoons

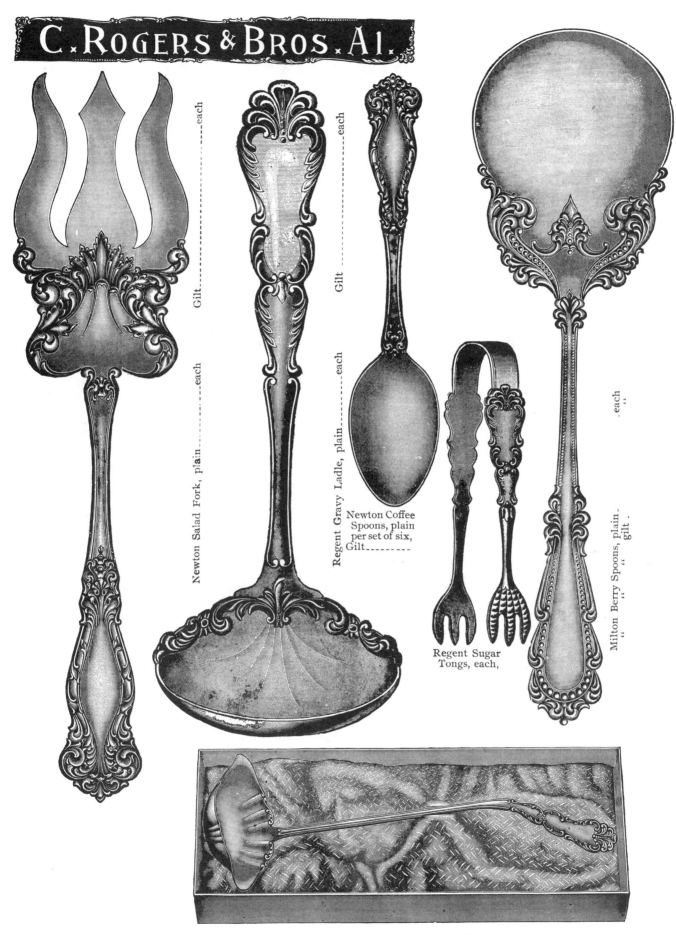

C. ROGERS & BROS. A1.

Gilt .... each

Gilt .... each

Newton Salad Fork, plain .... each

Regent Gravy Ladle, plain .... each

Newton Coffee
Spoons, plain
per set of six,
Gilt ....

Regent Sugar
Tongs, each,

Milton Berry Spoons, plain
" " gilt .

......each
" "

Regent Punch Ladle, plain .

Gold Bowl .

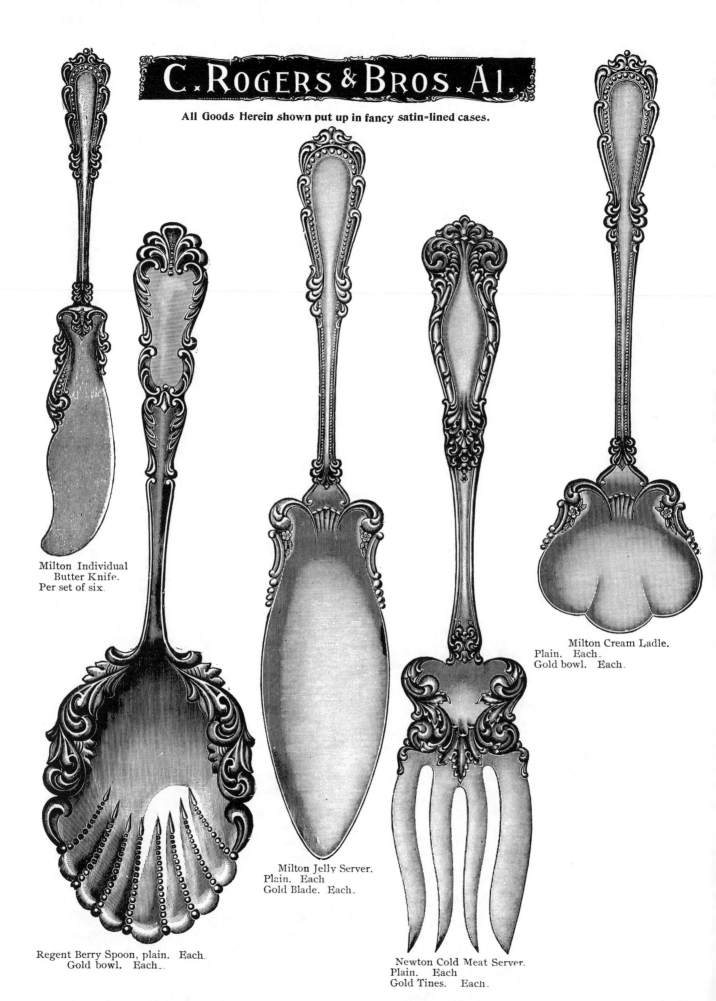

C. ROGERS & BROS. A1.

All Goods Herein shown put up in fancy satin-lined cases.

Milton Individual
Butter Knife.
Per set of six.

Regent Berry Spoon, plain.   Each.
Gold bowl.   Each.

Milton Jelly Server.
Plain.   Each
Gold Blade.   Each.

Newton Cold Meat Server.
Plain.   Each
Gold Tines.   Each.

Milton Cream Ladle.
Plain.   Each.
Gold bowl.   Each.

Put Up in Fancy Satin Lined Boxes.

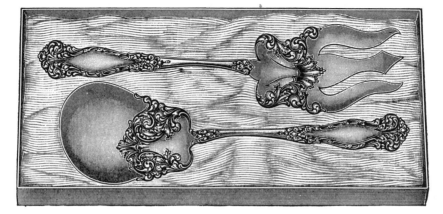

Newton Salad Set, plain
" " " gilt

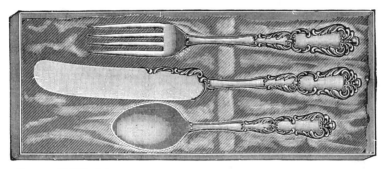

Regent Child's Set

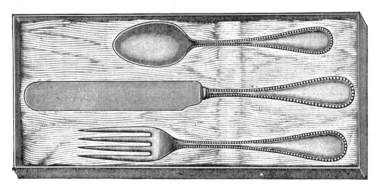

Plato Child's Set

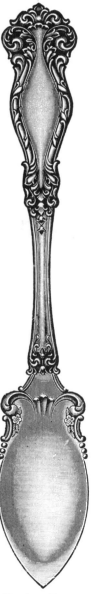

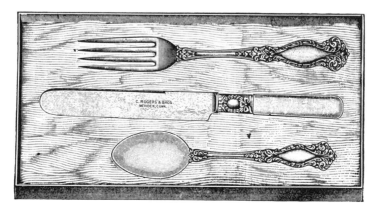

Newton Jelly Server.
Plain _____ each,
Gilt _____ "

Newton Child Set, pearl handle, Sterling silver ferrule ____ per set,

Newton Orange
Spoons. Plain, set
of 6 __ each,
Gilt ____ "

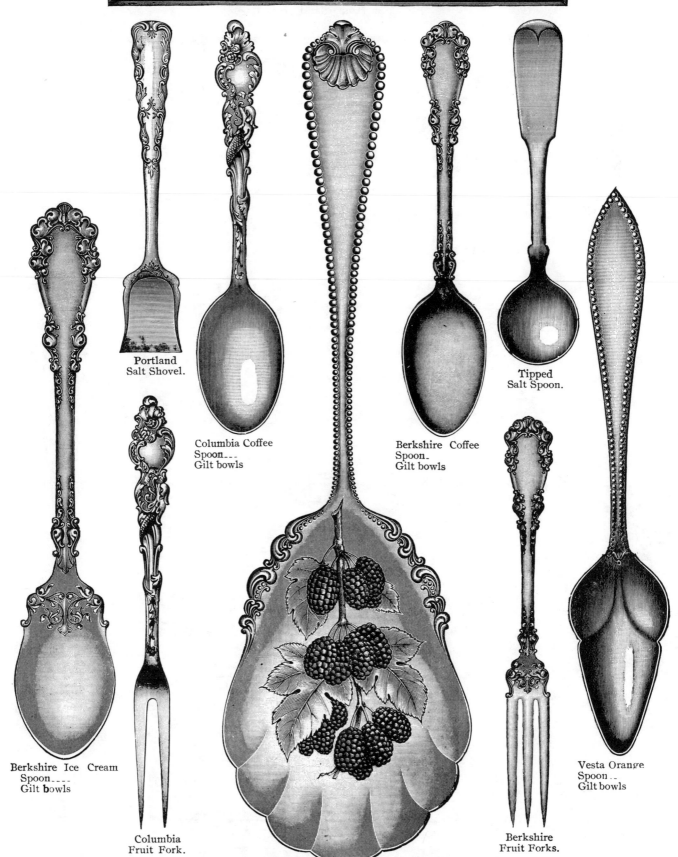

·1847·ROGERS BROS.

Portland
Salt Shovel.

Columbia Coffee
Spoon____
Gilt bowls

Berkshire Coffee
Spoon_
Gilt bowls

Tipped
Salt Spoon.

Berkshire Ice Cream
Spoon____
Gilt bowls

Columbia
Fruit Fork.

Berkshire
Fruit Forks.

Vesta Orange
Spoon__
Gilt bowls

Milan Berry Spoon, full chased bowl, extra plate,
Gold lined
XX Gold Inlaid

Wᵐ ROGERS, ★
Wallingford, Ct.

"Eagle Brand"

Sultana.

Melrose.

Yale.

York.

Blenheim.

Tipped.

Price List for Above Patterns.

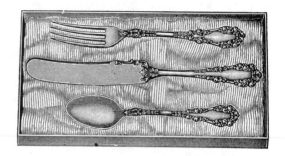

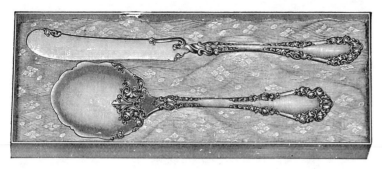

No. 604   Berkshire Butter Knife and Sugar Shell in lined box .

No. 116   Berkshire Child Set of Three
Pieces

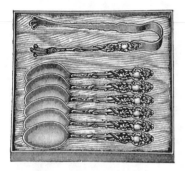

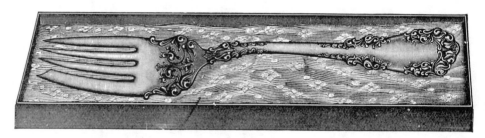

No. 705   Columbia.   One
Sugar Tong and Six Coffee
Spoons.................
Berkshire, Vesta, Lotus, Savoy and
Portland, same price.

Berkshire Cold Meat Fork in lined box
"   "   "   "   gilt tines, in lined box .

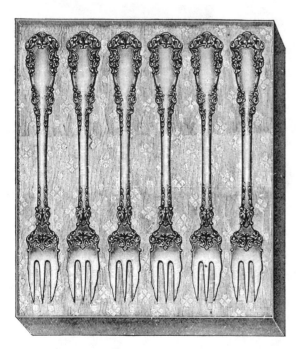

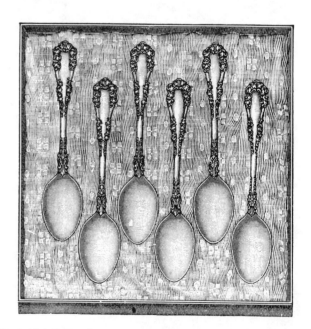

Berkshire Oyster Forks.

Berkshire Coffee Spoons.
"   "   "   gilt bowls.

102

W⁎ROGERS,★
Wallingford, Ct.

"Eagle Brand"

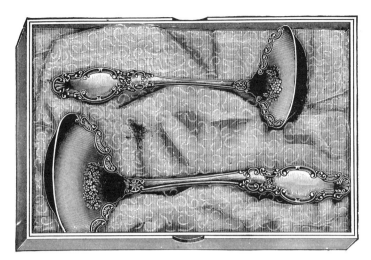

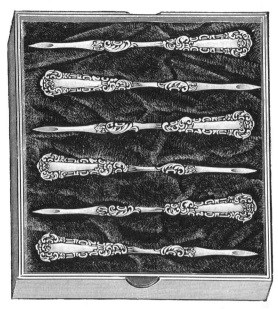

No. 152. Flat Ware combination. Melrose gravy and Cream
    ladles. In silk-lined box-------------------------------
    Gold lined--------- ------------------------------------
            Also Yale and Blenheim.

Yale Nut Picks, extra plate-------------------
        Also furnished in Melrose pattern.

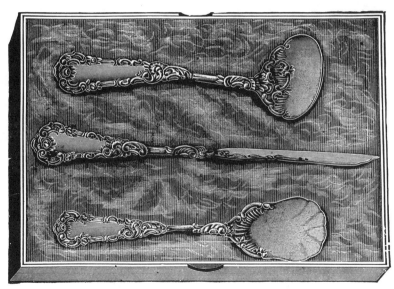

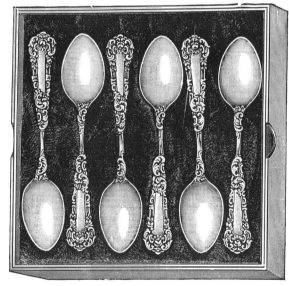

No. 153 Flat Ware combination. Yale Sugar Shell, Butter Knife and
Cream Ladle---
       Also Blenheim, Melrose and York.

Yale Coffee Spoons, plain bowl--------------
   "   "   " gilt " --------------

Yale Jelly Shell, plain --------------------------
   "   "   " gilt------------------------------
   "   "   "   " bright cut--------------------
     Also furnished in Melrose and Blenheim.

W*ROGERS,★ Wallingford, Ct.   "*Eagle Brand*"

Blenheim Cold Meat Fork, large size, gold tines
Each in fancy white lined box.

Benheim Coffee Spoons.
Plain bowls,
Gold bowls,
Packed ½ doz. in fancy
lined box. Furnished
in all patterns.

Melrose Cold Meat Fork, large size, gold tines
Each in fancy lined box; also furnished in Yale and Seville pattern.

Blenheim Jelly Shell.
Silver Bowl
Gold bowl
Bright cut and gold bowl
Each in fancy white lined box.

Melrose Jelly Shell
Silver Bowl
Gold bowl
Bright cut and gold bowl
Each in fancy white lined box;
also furnished in Yale pattern.

SILVER PLATED FLATWARE.

Silver plated on 10 per cent nickel silver.   Made by C. Rogers & Bro. and stamped R. S. P. Co.   Being hand burnished, they are equal in appearance and finish to the finest goods made.

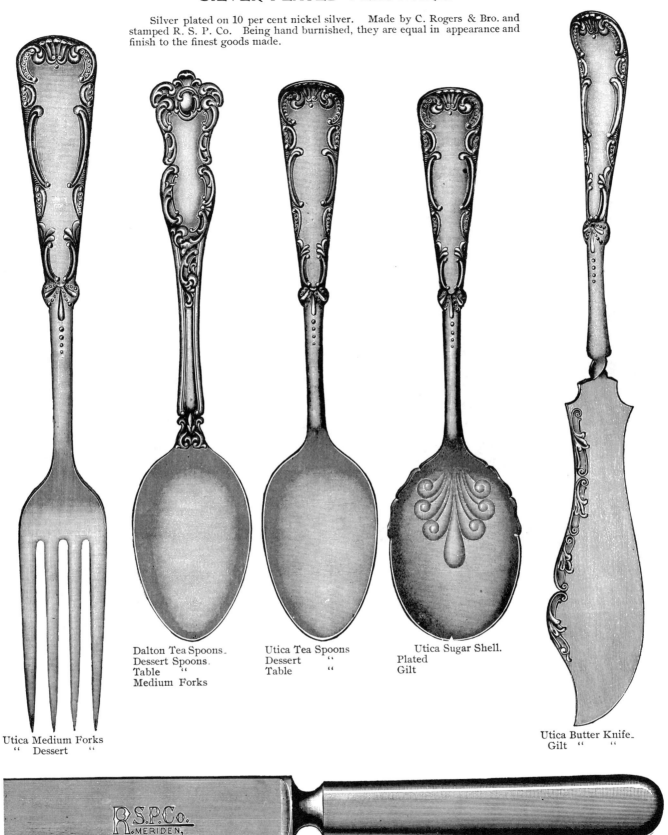

Utica Medium Forks
" Dessert "

Dalton Tea Spoons.
Dessert Spoons.
Table   "
Medium Forks

Utica Tea Spoons
Dessert   "
Table   "

Utica Sugar Shell.
Plated
Gilt

Utica Butter Knife.
Gilt   "   "

R. S. P. Co.'s Medium Knife.

No. 2502   Steel Medium Knives and Forks, round end plain.
No. 2503   "   Dessert   "   "   "   "   "   "

C. ROGERS & BROS. A1.

Put up in fancy satin lined boxes.

Regent Individual Salad Fork...

Newton Gravy Ladle plain...
"   "   gilt...

Newton Sugar Tongs...

Newton Pie Knife, plain...
"   "   gilt...

Newton Berry Fork, plain...

W. F. ROGERS BRAND OF FLATWARE.

A1 Plate 18% Nickel Sliver Base.

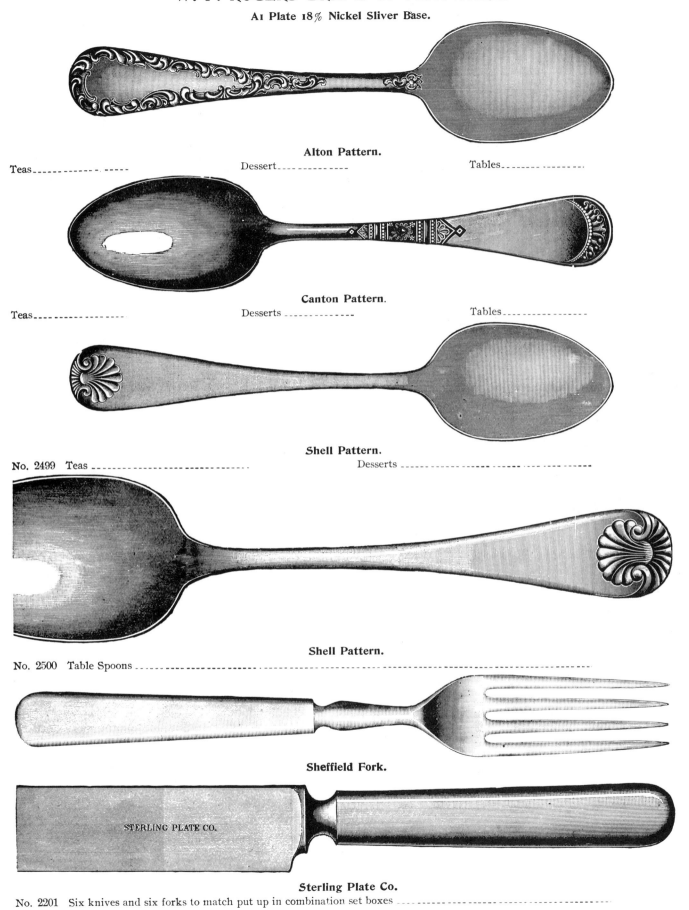

Alton Pattern.

Teas_____   Dessert_____   Tables_____

Canton Pattern.

Teas_____   Desserts_____   Tables_____

Shell Pattern.

No. 2499   Teas_____   Desserts_____

Shell Pattern.

No. 2500   Table Spoons_____

Sheffield Fork.

STERLING PLATE CO.

Sterling Plate Co.

No. 2201   Six knives and six forks to match put up in combination set boxes_____

107

All fancy pieces, put up in fancy lined boxes.

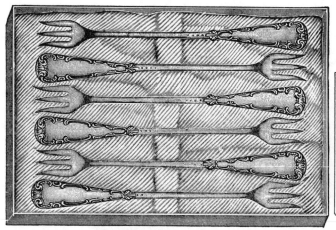

Utica Oyster Forks, per set of six

Utica Child's Set

Utica Berry Spoon, plain.
Gilt bowl

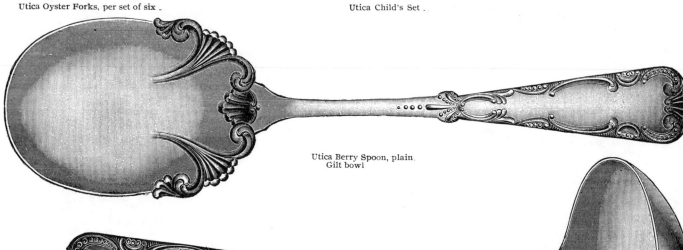

Utica Gravy Ladle, plain.
Gilt.

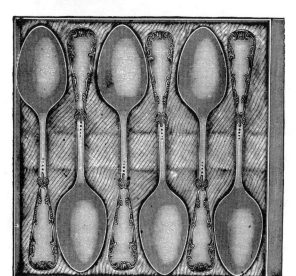

Utica Coffee Spoons, plain, per set of six
Gilt bowl, per set of six.

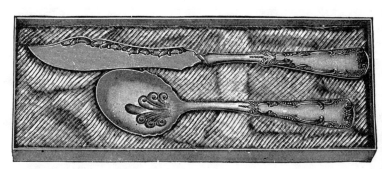

Utica Butter Knife and Sugar Shell Set.
With gilt bowl sugar shell

Quadruple Silver Plated Coffee Sets.

Coffee Set. Plain Burnished. Four Pieces, including Tray. Cream Gold Lined. Pot has Ebony Handle.
No. 8651

Coffee Set. Bright Finished. Four Pieces, including Tray. Cream Gold Lined. Pot has Ebonized Handle.
No. 8652

SILVER PLATED WARE.

No. **5955**.   Tea, Satin Engraved, Height 7¼ in

No. **5963**.   Tea, Fluted, Burnished

No. **5931**.   Tea, Chased and Burnished

Tea.
No. 8630

No. **5937**.   Tea Pot, Plain, Polished, Height
8½ in., Capacity 5½ Half Pints

Tea.
No. 8628

DERBY SILVER PLATE CO.

Quadruple Plate.

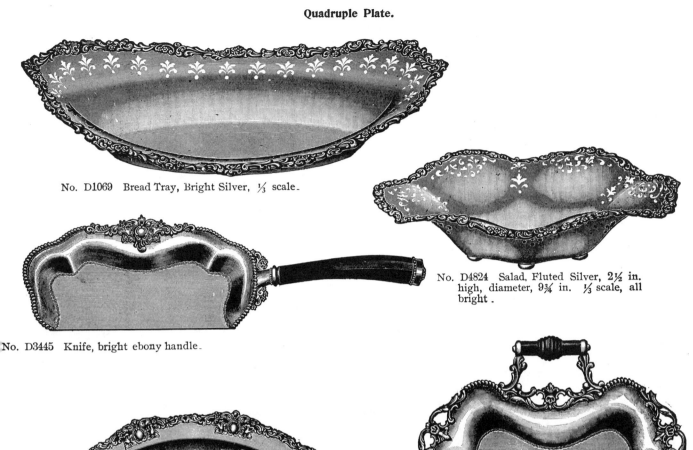

No. D1069   Bread Tray, Bright Silver, ⅓ scale.

No. D4824   Salad, Fluted Silver, 2½ in. high, diameter, 9¾ in. ⅓ scale, all bright.

No. D3445   Knife, bright ebony handle.

No. D3445   Tray, bright ebony handle.

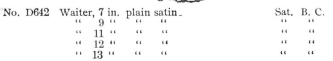

No. D642   Waiter, 7 in.   plain satin   Sat.   B. C.
     "   9 "   "   "   "   "
     " 11 "   "   "   "   "
     " 12 "   "   "   "   "
     " 13 "   "   "   "   "

No. D4817   Salad, Fluted Silver, 4¼ in. high, diameter 10 in. ⅓ scale.

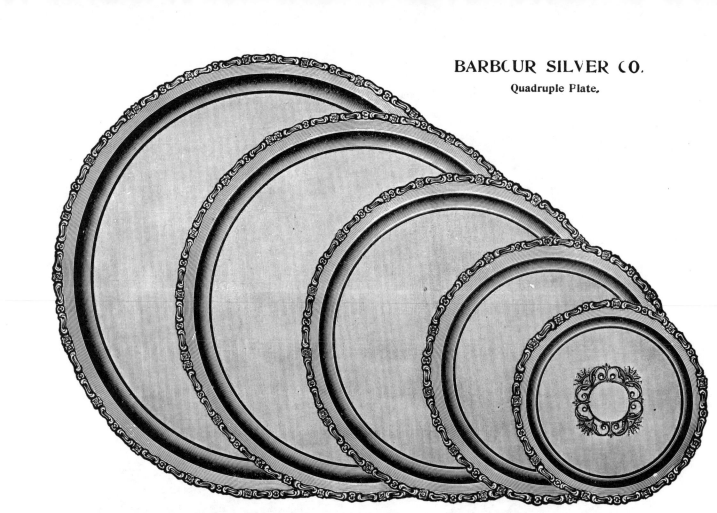

No. B523 Waiters, rococco border, satin, bright cut engraved center, 6 in.,   8 in ,   , 10 in.,   , 12 in.,   , 14 in.,

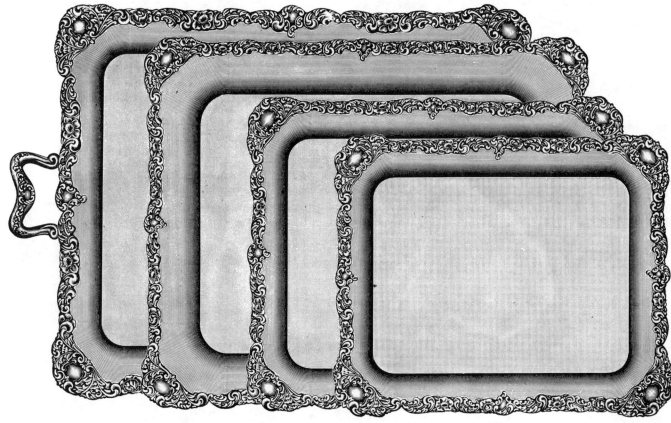

No. B221 Waiter, embossed border, 13 in., no handles,   , 15 in., no handles,   , 18 in., no handles,   , 18 in., with handles,   , 20 in., with handles,   , 24 in., with handles ---------------------------

No. B 2 21 Bread Tray. Satin,
  B. C., engraved
        Length, 13 inches.

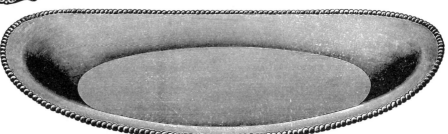

No. B 55 Bread Tray. Plain, bur-
  burnished.
  Satin
        Length, 13 inches.

No. B 2522 Bread Tray
  Satin, B. C. Length, 13 inches.

No. B 2067 Bon Bon. Satin, B. C., gold lined
        Diameter, 5 inches.

No. B 28 Bon Bon. Plain, burnished, gold lined
        Diameter, 6 inches.

No. B 25 Bon Bon. Plain, burnished, gold lined
        Diameter, 5 inches.

BARBOUR SILVER CO.
Quadruple Plate.

No. B2312. Two pieces, golden Lined_____
Mug, plain, height ¾ in. _____
Brush, plain_____

No. B20 Safety Match Holder
with matches; height 3½ in.

No. B2309 Two pieces, gold lined_____
Mug. Satin B. C., height, 3½ in___
Brush, plain_____

No. B16 Liquor Flask, Satin
B. C., height, 6 in_____

No. B2313 Two pieces gold lined_____
Mug, satin B. C., height, 3 in_____
Brush, plain_____

Glass Flask, leather covered.
Cup, satin, B. C., gold lined.
No. B13 ¼ Pint_____
No. B14 ½ " _____
No. B15 ¾ " _____

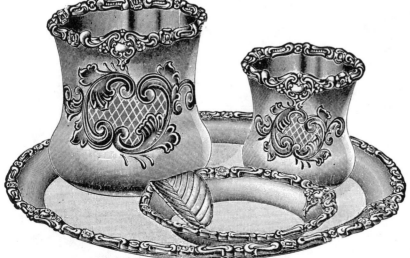

No. B2180 Smoking Set, 4 pieces, satin, B. C., gold lined, diameter, tray 8½ in.
height, cigar holder, 3½ in_____

No. B2169 Cigar or Tobacco Jar,
Satin, B. C.; height, 6¾ in.

No. B 2001   Curling Set.
Folding Irons with Ebony Handles.   All closes up in box for
traveling.   S ze, when closed, 3 x 6½.

No. B 9   Jewel Box
Bright embossed, satin lined.   Length, 6¼ in.

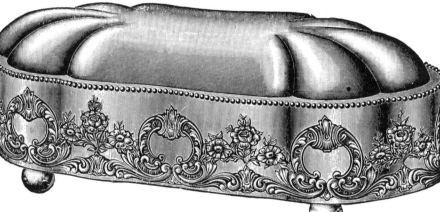

No. B 5   Pin Box
Size, 2 x 3½ inches.

No. B 11   Jewel or Glove Box
Bright embossed, satin lined.   Length, 11 inches.

No. B 6   Trinket or Jewel Box, plush lined
Size, 5 x 3 inches.

No. B 10   Jewel or Handkerchief Box
Bright embossed, satin lined.   6½ inches square.

BARBOUR
SILVER
CO.

Quadruple Plate.

No. B2079   Card Receiver; Plain; Height, 3 in......

No. B2080   Card Receiver; Satin, B. C.; Height 9 in ....

No. B11   Pin Tray; Length, 7¼ in ....

No. B2078   Card Receiver; Height, 6 in..........

No. B10   Pin Tray; Length, 5 in ....

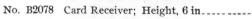

No. B236 Trinket Tray; Satin, B C., Burn'd Flange; Length, 6¼ in...

No. B235   Card Tray; Satin Center, Burnished Sides; Length, 6½ in ....

No. B12   Pin Tray; Length, 7½ in.................

BARBOUR SILVER CO.

QUADRUPLE PLATE.

No. B18   Coffee Set, 4 pieces, satin B. C.   Engraved
Coffee   Sugar, gold lined   Cream, gold lined.   Waiter, 10 inches.
Height Coffee, 8¾ inches.

No. B2421   3 pieces, plain burnished.
Sugar.   Cream, gold lined.   Spoon, gold lined.
Height Sugar, 5½ inches.

No. B2420   3 pieces, satin B. C.   Engraved.
Sugar   Cream, gold lined   Spoon, gold lined
Height, sugar 5½ inches.

Quadruple Plate.

No. B. 31   Spoon Tray, gold lined, satin, B. C.
Length, 10¾ inches.

No. B 64   Syrup, satin, B. C. engraved.
Height, 5 inches.

No. B 778   Tete-a-Tete Set.   3 pieces, satin, B. C., engraved
Engraved Coffee,   Sugar,   Cream, gold lined,   ;   Height, Coffee, 5½ in.

No. B 60 Cut glass, syrup. $3.00
Height, 4¾ inches.

No. B 2421 Syrup, satin, B. C., engraved
Height, 4¾ inches.

No. B 2422 Syrup, satin, B. C., engraved
Height, 5 inches.

No. B 62 Cut glass, syrup.
Height, 5 inches.

No. B 2423   Syrup, plain, burnished
Height, 5 inches.

No. B 29   Spoon Tray, satin, gold lined.
Length, 9 inches.

118

BARBOUR SILVER CO.

Quadruple Plate.

No. B2422   Tea Set; 5 pieces, satin B. C., engraved.
Coffee.   Tea.   Sugar.   Cream, gold lined.
Height, **Coffee**, 7 inches.   Spoon, gold lined.   Butter   Syrup

No. B2423   Tea Set; 5 pieces, plain burnished
Coffee   Tea.   Sugar   Cream, gold lined.   Spoon, gold lined.
Height, **Coffee**, 8 inches.   Urn or Swing Kettle.   Butter.   Syrup.

Quadruple Plate.

No. B 2419   Tea Set, 5 pieces, satin, B. C., engraved
    Coffee,   Tea,   Sugar   Cream gold lined,   Spoon, gold lined, $5.25 ;
    Height, Coffee, 7½ inches ;   Butter,   Syrup,

No. B 2421   Tea Set, 5 pieces, satin, B. C., engraved
    Coffee,   Tea,   ;   Sugar,   Cream, gold lined,   Spoon, gold lined,   ;
    Height, Coffee, 7½ inches ;   Butter,   Syrup,

No W **663** Tea Set. **6** pieces, complete
  Satin bright cut, cream and spoon gold lined   Tea Pot,   , height, **7¼** in., capacity, **4½** half pints ; Sugar   , height, **6** in. ;   Cream,   , height, **3⅝** in. ;
                    Spoon,   height, **3⅝** in. ; Butter,   , height, **5⅛** in. ; Syrup,   , height, **5¼** in.

No. W **68** Tea Set. **5** pieces
  Burnished, gold lined, Cream and Spoon Holder.   Coffee,   , capacity, **6** half pints, height, **9¾** inches ;   Sugar   , height, **6¾** inches ;   Tea,   capacity
    5 half pints, height, **8½** inches ;   Spoon,   height, **4½** inches ; Cream,   height, **4½** inches.

GUARANTEED QUADRUPLE PLATE SILVER WARE.
Manufactured by E. G. Webster & Son.

Tea; capacity, 2 half pints; height, 5½ in.,   Sugar; height, 2½ inches _____   Cream; height, 2½ inches ___$

No. W19 Tete-a-Tete Set, 3 pieces complete; Plain Burnished _____

Cream and Sugar Gold Lined.

Cream; height, 5 inches _____   Spoon Holder; height, 5 inches___   Sugar; height, 6¾ inches____

No. W62 Dessert Set 3 pieces complete; Fluted, Burnished _____

Cream and Spoon Holder Gold Lined.

Coffee; height, 8¾ in___   Sugar; height, 3½ in_   Cream; height, 4 in_   No. W220 Chocolate Pot; bur-

Tray,   dimensions 9½x9½ inches.   nished _____

No. W69 Coffee Set, 4 pieces, Burnished _____   Cut One Third Size.

Sugar and Cream Gold Lined.

SILVER PLATED WARE.

Coffee.
No. 8630

No. **5932**. Coffee, Chased and Burnished

No. **5956**. Coffee, Satin Engraved, Height 8 in

No. **5981**. Coffee, Satin Shield

Coffee.
No. 8628

SILVER PLATED WARE.

Illustrations One-Third Size.

No. **5953**. Sugar, Satin Engraved

Sugar.
No. **8630**

No. **5959**. Sugar, Fluted, Burnished

No. **5929**. Sugar, Chased and Burnished

No. **5935**. Sugar Bowl, Plain, Polished. Height 6¼ in

No. **5987**. Sugar, Satin Shield

No. **5977**. Sugar, Satin Shield

Sugar.
No. **8628**

SILVER PLATED WARE.

No. **5952**. Cream, Satin Engraved, Gold
Lined

No. **5958**. Cream, Fluted, Burnished
Gold Lined

No. **5930**. Creamer, Chased and Burnished, Gold Lined

No. **5936**. Cream Pitcher, Plain, Polished,
Gold Lined, Height 5 in

No. **5984**. Cream, Satin Shield, Gold
Lined

Cream. Gold Lined.
No. **8630**

No. **5978**. Cream, Satin Shield, Gold
Lined

Cream. Gold Lined.
No. **8628**

Quadruple Silver Plated Syrup and Plates.

Syrup and Plate.   Plain Burnished.
No. **8646**

Syrup and Plate.   Plain Burnished.
No. **8636**

Syrup and Plate.   Bright Finish.
No. **8631**

No. **6027.**   Syrup and Plate, Satin Engraved, One-third Size.

No. **6024.**   Syrup and Plate, Burnished

SILVER PLATED WARE.

SYRUPS AND PLATES.

Illustrations One-Third Size

No. **6023.** Syrup and Plate, Embossed Satin

No. **6026.** Syrup and Plate, Satin Shield

No. **6028.** Syrup and Plate, Plain Burnished, Embossed, Height 5¼ in

No. **6030.** Syrup and Plate, Satin, Bright Cut, Engraved, Height 5¼ in

No. **6022.** Syrup and Plate, Burnished

No. **6029.** Syrup and Plate, Satin Shield

No. **6025.** Syrup and Plate, Chased and Burnished

No. **6021.** Syrup and Plate, 1-3 Size, Burnished

SILVER PLATED WARE.

Illustrations One-third Size.

No. 2055. BUTTER DISH. Height 7½ inches.

No. 2054. BUTTER DISH. Height 7½ inches.

No. 5961. Butter, Fluted, Burnished

No. 5988. Butter Dish, Satin Shield.

No. 5980. Butter Dish, Satin Shield

Butter Dish.
No. 8630

Butter Dish. Burnished, Cut-glass Drainer.
No. 8628

No. **6005**. Butter Dish, Burnished, Cut Glass Drainer

No. **6006**. Butter Dish, Satin Bright Cut Engraved, Glass Drainer. Height 5 inches.

No. **6004**. Butter Dish, Satin, B. C. Engraved, Glass Drainer

No. **6003**. Butter Dish, Burnished

No. **6009**. Butter Dish, Chased and Burnished.

No. **6007**. Butter Dish, Burnished, Height 6⅜ inches

No. **6008**. Butter Dish, Satin, B. C. Engraved, Glass Drainer, Height 5¼ inches

SILVER PLATED WARE.
Illustrations One-third Size.

No. 2051. SPOON HOLDER. Height, 5½ inches

SPOON HOLDER. Height, 6 inches.

No. 2050. SPOON HOLDER. Height, 6½ inches.

No. 2053. SPOON HOLDER. Height, 6 inches.

No. 5954. Spoon Holder, Satin Engraved Gold Lined

No. 5979. Spoon, Satin Shield, Gold Lined

No. 5928. Spooner, Chased and Burnished, Gold Lined

No. 5934. Spoon Holder, Plain, Polished, Gold Lined, Height 5 in

Spoon Holder. Gold Lined. No. 8630

No. 5960. Spooner, Fluted, Burnished, Gold Lined

No. 5986. Spoon Holder, Satin Shield, Gold Lined

Spoon Holder. Gold Lined. No. 8628

SILVER PLATED WARE.
WATER SETS AND PITCHERS.

Illustrations One-Third Size.

Prices Each.

No. 6329. Water Pitcher, burnished, fluted and beaded, capacity 9 half pints, height 7½ inches .

No. 6327. Tilting Water Set, satin, bright cut, engraved, gold lined goblets. height 18½ inches. capacity 5 pints

Ice Pail. Burnished.
No. 8813.

No. 6331. Water Set, 3 pieces, burnished, gold lined goblet, complete

SILVER PLATED WARE.
WATER SETS AND PITCHERS.
Illustrations One-third Size.

No. **6325**. Ice Pitcher, Satin Engraved. Burnished Shield, Porcelain Lined, One-third Scale.

No. **6337**. Water Pitcher, Silver Lined, Capacity, 1½ Quarts.

No. **6323**. Tilting Water Set, Bright Silver, Fluted, Goblet and Waste Bowl Gold Lined, Height 20 in.

No. **6324**. Pitcher, Satin B. C., Porcelain Lined, One-third Scale, Height 12 in.

GUARANTEED QUADRUPLE PLATE SILVERWARE.

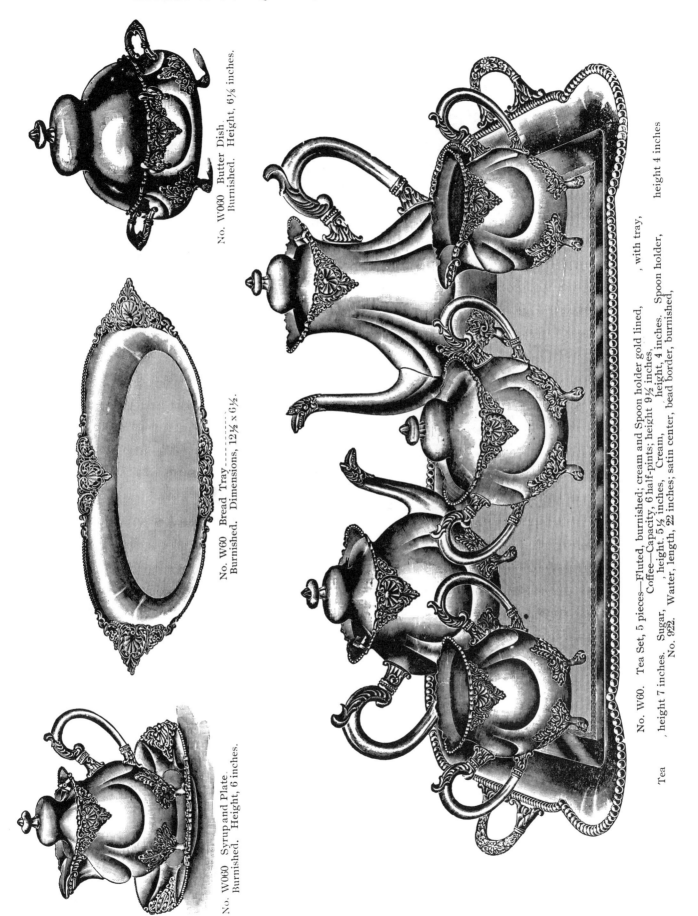

No. W060 Butter Dish.
Burnished. Height, 6⅛ inches.

No. W60 Bread Tray ....
Burnished. Dimensions, 12½ x 6½.

No. W060 Syrup and Plate.
Burnished. Height, 6 inches.

No. W60. Tea Set, 5 pieces—Fluted, burnished; cream and Spoon holder gold lined, , with tray,
Coffee—Capacity, 6 half-pints; height 9½ inches,
, height. 5½ inches, Cream, height, 4 inches. Spoon holder, height 4 inches
No. 922. Waiter, length, 22 inches; satin center, bead border, burnished,
Tea , height 7 inches. Sugar,

No. B 2170 Candelabra. 5 light
Plain. Height, 12½ inches.

No. B 2169 Candlestick
Plain. Height, 11 inches.

No. B 2163½ Candlestick.
Plain. Height, 11 inches.

No. B 2162 Candelabra. 5 light
Plain. Height, 13 inches.

No. A0293 Tea Set, five pieces, plain ....   Embossed ....
Plain, Coffee ....   Tea ....   Sugar __ $5 50; Cream, gold lined ....   Spoon, gold lined ..
Embossed, Coffee ....   Tea ....   Sugar __ 6.50; Cream, gold lined ..   Spoon, gold lined ..
No. A0293, Waiter,

No. A0293 Butter, plain....   No. A0293 Urn; plain,   Embossed,   No. A0293 Syrup, plain ....
Embossed ---------   Embossed ....

GUARANTEED QUADRUPLE PLATE SILVERWARE.

Manufactured by E. G. Webster & Son.

No. W157 Cake Basket
Burnished, bright cut engraved satin center.
Length 12½ inches.   Height 7¾ inches.

No. W159 Cake Basket.
Fluted, burnished.   Diameter, 9¾ inches.   Height, 7¾ inches.

No, W608 Cake Basket, burnished
Height, 9½ inches.   Diameter 9⅛ inches.

No. W158 Cake, silver lined   **No. W158 Gold lined**
Satin bright cut, rose border.   Height 8½ inches.   Diameter 9¼ inches.

No. W615 Cake Basket.
Plain burnished.   Height 9½ inches.   Diameter 9¾ inches.

No. W0613 Cake Basket.
Burnished, height 9 inches.   Diameter of bowl 10½ x 8¾ inches.

No. M027   Berry Dish.
Colored glass.
With pink glass

No. M333   Berry Dish.
Colored glass.

No. M024.   Berry Dish.
Colored glass.

No. M026   Berry Dish.
Colored glass.
With pink glass

No. M 143 Bon Bon. Satin finish,
gold lined ----------------------

No. M 131 Spoon Tray. Satin finish, engraved----------------

No. M 024 Bread Tray. Satin finish,
engraved ----------------------------

No. M 025 Bread Tray. Satin finish,
engraved ----------------------

No. M 023 Bread Tray. Satin finish, hand
engraved, Rococo border-------------------

No. M 021 Bread Tray. Satin engraved, beaded border---------

No. M 130 Spoon or Card Tray. Satin finish,
engraved, beaded border---------------

QUADRUPLE PLATE SILVERWARE.

No. A815   Coffee Set, 4 piece complete, hand engraved, gold
lined.

No. A55   Water Pitcher, 3 qt. with fender
No. A56   "   "   1 "   no   "

No. A30 Napkin Ring, em-
bossed.

No. A69   Cheese Dish, hand engraved, crystal dish.

No. A1   Napkin Ring,
hand engraved.

No. A67   Cracker Jar, hand engraved

No A 813 Tooth Pick Holder, decorated glass.

No. A56   Combination Sugar, hand
burnished.

139

No. M034 Cake Basket, satin finish, engraved,
rococo border, plain center.

No. M038 Cake Basket, Satin finish, engraved,
rococo border.

No. M037 Cake Basket, satin finish, engraved,
rococo border.

No. M0606 Cake Basket, satin engraved,
Gold lined.

MANHATTAN SILVER PLATE CO.

No. M022 Berry Dish __
                Crystal Glass.

No. M023 Berry Dish __
                Crystal Glass.

No. M418 Berry Dish ___
                Crystal Glass.

No. M025 Berry Dish __
                Colored Glass.

MANHATTAN SILVER PLATE CO.

No. M014 SOUP TUREEN.
Capacity 3, quarts; Satin Finish; Beaded Border

No. M013 SOUP TUREEN.
Satin Finish; Hand Engraved; Rococo Border; Holds 3 quarts, each

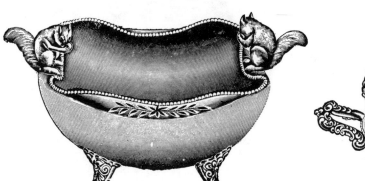

No. M120 NUT BOWL.
Satin Finish; Gold Lined; Beaded Border

No. M211 BAKING DISH.
Satin Finish; Hand Engraved; Rococo Border

No. M212 BAKING DISH.
Satin Engraved

No. M121 NUT BOWL.
Satin Finish; Gold Lined; Rococo Border

No. M0107 Crumb Set, satin fiuish. Engraved,

No. M0108 Crumb Set. Satin finish, engraved,

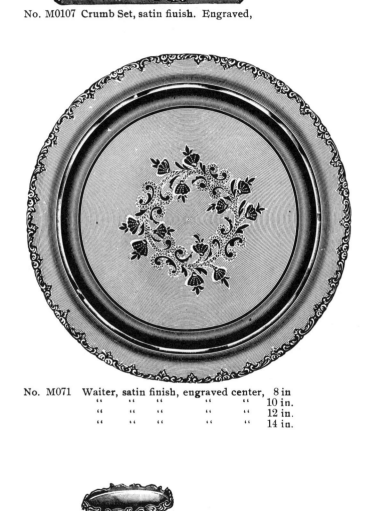

No. M071   Waiter, satin finish, engraved center,   8 in
    "   "   "   "   "   10 in.
    "   "   "   "   "   12 in.
    "   "   "   "   "   14 in.

No. M0109   Crumb Set.   Satin finish, en-
    graved.

No. M110 Smoking Set.   Four pieces, gold lined; satin
    finish, engraved.

No. M111 Smoking Set.   Four pieces; satin finish, hand
    engraved, gold lined.

No. W31   Flower Pot
Burnished, crock lining.   Height, 4 inches.

No. W0401 Vase
Burnished.   Height 5⅜ inches.

No W59   Bon Bon
Satin gold lined.   Diameter 5 inches.

No. W20   Jug
Cut glass effect.
Height 11¼ inches.   Capacity 2 quarts.

No. W399   Vase
Burnished crystal glass.
Height 10¼ inches.

No. W331   Tooth Pick Holder.
Repousse, silver, gold lined
"   gold enamel

No. W **140** Bowl. Plain burnished _____
Height, 2¾ inches; diameter, 8½ inches.

No. W **139** Bowl. Fluted, burnished, silver lined_____
Diameter, 8⅛ inches.

No. W **36** Fern Dish. Burnished, pierced body, pottery lining,
green enamel. Height, 4¼ in.; diameter, 7 in._____

No. W **27** Fern Dish. Burnished, white enamel, porcelain lining.
Height, 4½ inches; diameter, 7 inches _____

No. W **662** Butter Dish. Satin bright cut, fluted and burnished.
Height, 4½ inches _____

No. W **87** Syrup. Cut glass, burnished. Height, 3½ inches_____

No. W **92** Syrup and Plate. Plain satin burnished shield. Height, 5¼ inches_____

No. W **68** Syrup. Burnished. Height, 6
inches _____

No. W **662** Syrup and Plate Satin bright
cut, fluted and burnished. Height, 3¾ in

QUADRUPLE PLATE SILVERWARE.

No. A811   Berry Dish
Crystal Glass.

No. A812   Berry Dish
Rose and Crystal Glass.

No A96   Fruit Dish
Fine Crystal Glass.

No. A408   Jelly or Preserve Dish
Crystal Glass.

No. A11   Jelly or Preserve Dish
Crystal Glass.

QUADRUPLE PLATE SILVERWARE.

No. A104 Cup
Hand engraved, gold lined.

No. A204 Cup
Hand engraved, gold lined.

No A504 Cup
Hand engraved, gold lined.

No A410 Cup
Hand engraved, gold lined.

No. A0 Salts. Per doz.
Self righting.

No. A809 Shaving Mug and brush
Hand engraved, gold lined.

No. A813 Shaving Mug and Brush
Embossed, gold lined.

No. A10.
Salts and Peppers.

No. A14.
Hand engraved.

No. A13.
In neat box; per pair

GUARANTEED QUADRUPLE PLATE SILVERWARE.

No W191 Fruit, plain pink opal bowl, height, 15 inches.
With gold decorated bowl

No. W1ᶜ9 Fruit Dish, burnished with pink or green, opal
lined bowl, gold decorated on outside and inside,
height, 14 inches, diameter of bowl, 11 inches

No. W182 Fruit Stand, crystal glass, height 12¼ in; Diam. 8¼ in.

No W163 Fruit, Pink opal bowl, height 10 inches

Quadruple Silver Plated Water Set

Water Pitcher. Satin Engraved.
No. **8809** .

Water Set. 3 Pieces. Fluted and Burnished.
Pitcher .   Goblet .   Tray .
No. **8810.** Set complete .

Water Set. 4 Pieces. Satin Engraved.
Pitcher .   Slop Bowl, Gold Lined .
Goblet , Gold Lined .   Tray, Satin
No. **8811.** Set complete .

Water Pitcher. Satin Engraved.
No. **8812** .

SILVER PLATED WARE.

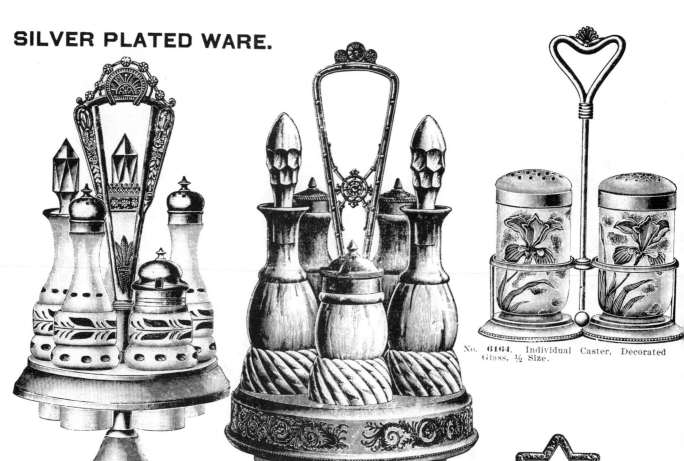

No. **6139**. Caster, 5 Bottles, Plain, Height 15½ in.

No. **6164**. Individual Caster, Decorated Glass, ½ Size.

No. **6140**. Caster, 5 Bottles, No. 14 Bottles, Chased, One-third size.

Individual Caster. Decorated Bottles. No. **8840**.

Breakfast Caster. Tinted Bottles. Burnished Pierced Frame. No. **8841**.

No. **6141**. Caster, Chased.

SILVER PLATED WARE.

No. **6136**. With No. 2 Bell Handle, Chased, 5 No. 14 Bottles, One-third size.

No. **6137**. Breakfast or Lunch Caster, 3 Cut Glass Bottles, Height 6½ in.

No. **6167**. Individual or Lunch Caster, Crystal Glass .

No. **6138**. Caster, Satin, Bright Cut. 5 Engraved Bottles, Height 14½ in.

No. **6165**. Decorated Cruets, Half Size.

No. **6166**. Individual Caster, Crystal Bottles, Length 4¼ in., Height 4½ in.

Pickle Casters—Quadruple Silver Plated Frames.
CRYSTAL AND COLORED GLASS.

Pickle Caster.   Crystal Glass, Gold and Green Decoration.

No. **8832** .

Pickle Caster.   Crystal Glass.

No. **8833** .

Pickle Caster.   Colored Glass, with Gilt Decoration.

No. **8834** .

Pickle Caster.   Crystal Glass.

No. **8835** .

Pickle Caster.   Ruby Decorated Glass.

No. **8836** .

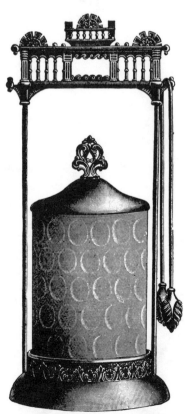

Pickle Caster.   Ruby Glass.

No. **8837** .

SILVER PLATED WARE.
CUPS.

No. **6470**. Cup, satin engraved, gold lined, burnished shield

No: **6471**. Cup, satin engraved, gilt.

No. **6472**. Cup, satin bright cut, engraved, gold lined, height 3 in.

No. **6473**. Cup, satin bright cut, engraved, gold lined, height 3 in.

No. **6474**. Cup, satin engraved, G. L.

No. **6475**. Cup, satin engraved, gold lined,

No. **6476**. Cup, satin engraved, gold lined, one-half size.

No. **6477**. Child's Cup, plain, gold lined, height 2 in.

No. **6478**. Cup, satin engraved, gold lined, burnished shield.

Satin Engraved. Gold Lined.
No. **8799**.

Satin Engraved, Gold Lined.
No. **8801**.

Satin Shield, Gold Lined.
No. **8797**.

Quadruple Silver Plated Cups and Cups and Saucers.

Illustrations One-Half Size.

No. **6467.** Cup, beaded, burnished, gold lined, height 3⅛ in.

No. **6468.** Cup, satin engraved, gold lined, burnished shield .

No. **6469.** Cup, S. B. C., burnished shield, gold lined .

Cup and Saucer. Burnished, Gold Lined.
No. 8787 .

Plain Polished, Gold Lined.
No. 8802 .

Fluted Burnished.
No. 8794 .

No. **8789.** Cup and Saucer. Gold Lined .
No. **8790.** Same, with Mustache Guard .

Collapsion Cup.
No. 8792 .

Embossed Burnished.
No. 8791 .

No. **8785.** Cup and Saucer. Satin Engraved
No. **8786.** Same, with Mustache Guard .

Collapsion Cup. In Leather Case.
No. 8788 .

Satin Engraved, Gold Lined.
No. 8796 .

SILVER PLATED WARE.

No. 6249. Berry Set, 3 Pieces, Satin Shield, Gold Lined .

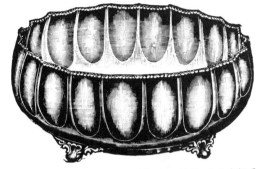

No. 6236. Bowl, fluted, beaded, burnished, gold lined, height 3 inches, diameter 7 inches.

No. 6237. Bowl, Butler finish, burnished center, French grey finish on new art trimmings, diameter 9¾ in. height 1⅝ in.

Illustration One-Third Size.

No. 6228. Nut or Fruit Bowl, fluted, gold lined, bright finished.

No. 6229. Nut Bowl, gold lined.

No. 6245. Berry Set, 3 Pieces, Burnished, Gold Lined

SILVER PLATED WARE.

Illustrations One-Third Size.

No. **6349**. Punch Set. with 12 Cups and Ladle.

No. **6360**. Wine Cooler, Burnished, Quart Size, Height 9½ in.....

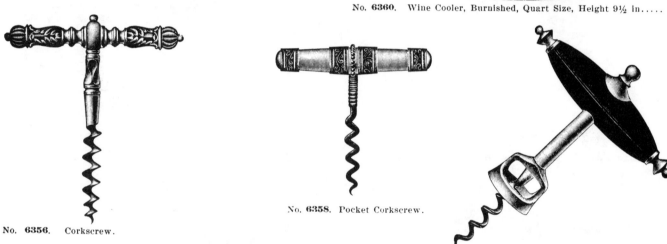

No. **6356**.   Corkscrew.

No. **6358**.   Pocket Corkscrew.

No. **6359**.   Self-pulling Cork-screw

No. **6361**.   Ice Tub, Plain Burnished, Height 4½ in.   Diameter 5½ inches .

No. **6355**.   Selp-pulling Corkscrew.

SILVER PLATED WARE.

SALT AND PEPPER SETS.

Pepper and Salt Shakers.   Fluted.
No. **8838** .

QUADRUPLE
SILVER PLATED

Pepper and Salt Shakers.   Fluted Burnished.
No. **8839** .

Illustration One-Half Size.

No. **6153**.   Table Salt and Peppers, Bright
Finished.

No. **6154**.   Salt and Pepper, Burnished, ½
Size.

No. **6155**.   Nickel Silver Salt and Pepper.
Glass Lined.

No. **6156**   Fluted Burnished.

No. **6157**.   Table Salt and Peppers, Bright
Finished.

No. **6158**.   Navy Salt and Pepper, 2 in box,
Satin.   Engraved

No. **6160**.   Salt Set, Burnished, Gold Lined.
Two Salts and Spoons, boxed.

No. **6161**.   Table Salt and Pepper. Fluted.

SILVER PLATED WARE.
TOOTH PICK HOLDERS.
Illustrations One-half Size.

No. **6551**. Pick Holder, pierced, burnished, gold lined, ½ size.

No. **6553**. Pick Holder, burnished, gold lined, ½ size,

No. **6552**. Pick Holder, black inlaid engraving, gold lined, ½ size .

No. **6545**. Pick Holder, pierced, burnished, gold lined, ½ size.

No. **6544**. Pick Holder, pierced, burnished, gold lined, ½ size.

Pick or Match Holder. Burnished, Gold Lined. No. **8857**

No. **6541**. Tooth Pick Holder, satin engraved, gold lined, full size. .

No. **6555**. Tooth Pick

No. **6548**. Tooth Pick Holder or Match Safe

No. **6554**. Tooth Pick or Match Holder

No. **6547**. Pick Holder, fluted .

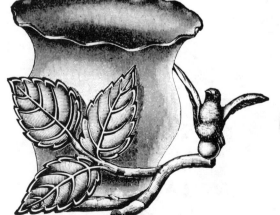

No. **6539**. Tooth Pick or Match Holder, satin, gold lined, full size.

No. **6550**. Tooth Pick Holder, satin engraved

Pick Holder. Burnished, Gold Lined. No. **8858**

BARBOUR SILVER CO.
Quadruple Plate.

No. B27 Napkin Ring; Plain, Chased; doz

Cut full size.

No. B103 Napkin Ring; Plain, Chased; doz

Cut full size.

No. B114 Napkin Ring; Satin, Bright Cut

Cut full size.

No. B135 Napkin Ring; Plain, Gold Lined; doz. Cut full size.

No. B137 Napkin Ring; Plain, Gold Lined; doz., Cut full size.

No. B139 Napkin Ring; Plain, Gold lined; doz., Cut full size.

No. B7 Napkin Ring; Satin, B. C., Gold Lined

Height, 2½ in.

No. B131 Napkin Ring; Satin. Bright Cut; doz

Cut full size.

No. B8 Napkin Ring; Satin, B. C., Gold Lined.

Height, 4 in.

No. B22 Tooth Pick Holder; Satin, B. C., Gold Lined
Height, 2 in.

No. B 67 Napkin Ring; Satin. B. C., Gold Lined
Height, 2½ in.

BARBOUR SILVER CO.

QUADRUPLE PLATE.

No. B5405   Childs Cup, triple
plate, satin B. C. gold lined
Height 2½ inches.

No. B5407   Child's Cup, triple plate,
satin B. C. gold lined.
Height 3 inches.

No. B5406   Child's Cup, triple plate,
satin B. C., gold lined..
Height 3 inches.

No. B112   Child's Cup, satin B. C.,
gold lined..
Height 3 inches.

No. B237   Child's Cup, satin B. C., gold
lined
Height 2 inches.

No. B113   Child's Cup, satin B. C.,
gold lined.
Height 3 inches.

No. B239   Child's Cup, satin B. C.,
gold lined
Height 3 inches.

No. B238   Child's Cup, plain embossed, gold lined .
Height, 2½ inches.

No. B240   Child's Cup, satin B. C.,
gold lined.
Height 3 inches.

No. B8   Cup and Saucer, gold lined plain burnished.
Height 3 inches.

No. B07   Moustache Cup and Saucer, satin B. C. gold lined.
Height 3 inches.

160

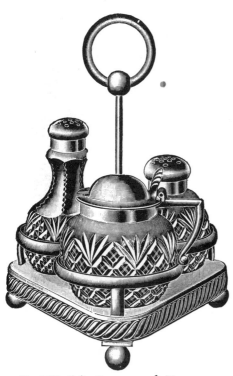

No. B55   Salt, Pepper, and Mustard Castor
Height 7 inches.

No. B50   Salt and Pepper Castor.
Height 7 inches.

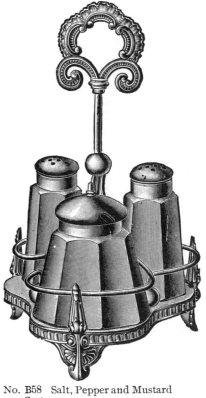

No. B58   Salt, Pepper and Mustard Castor.
Height 7¾ inches.

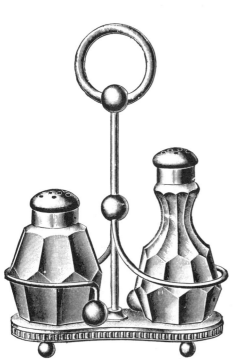

No. B61   Salt and Pepper Castor.
Height 6¼ inches.

No. B59   Salt, Pepper and Mustard Castor
Height 7 inches.

No. B49   Salt and Pepper Castor.
Pink and blue decorated bottles.
Height 6¾ inches.

BARBOUR SILVER CO.
Quadruple Plate.

No. B142 Pickle Caster, crystal decorated jar, height, 10 inches

No. B17 Marmalade or Jelly Dish, rose, buff shaded jar, gold decorations, height, 4¼ in.

No. B2309 Pickle Caster, crystal jar, height 11 in

No. B2315 Pickle Caster, ruby decorated, height 10 in

No. B16 Cracker Jar, buff and rose shaded jar, gold decorations, height without handle 7 in

No. B2316 Pickle Caster, ruby decorated, height 11 in

QUADRUPLE SILVER PLATED WARE.

No. 2064. CARD STAND. Height, 8 inches.

No. 2065. CARD STAND. Height. 7 inches.

Paperweight. French Grey Finish. Two-thirds size. No. 8855 .

No. 6723. Golf Trinket Box, gold lined, ½ size.

FLOWER HOLDER
Pierced; embossed; gray finish; height 4⅝ inches; diameter 6 inches.
B3510

No. 6714. Trinket Box, satin engraved, gold lined

Paperweight. French Grey Finish. Two-thirds size. No. 8852

No. 2066. CARD STAND. Height, 7 inches.

SILVER PLATED WARE.

JEWEL BOXES.

Illustrations About One-Half Size.

No. **6388**. Jewel Box, satin lined, French grey finish, length 6¼ in.

No. **6389**. Jewel Casket, embossed and burnished, satin lined, 5½ x 4¼ x 4½ in.

No. **6390**. Jewel Box, satin lined, French grey finish, length, oval 6¾ in.

No. **6391**. Jewel, satin lined, pierced and burnished, dimensions, 5¼ x 3¾ x 3¼ in.

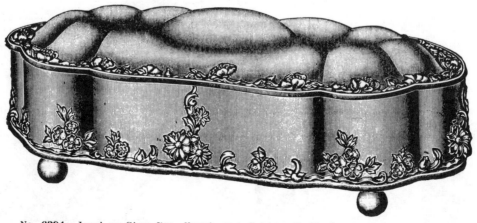

No. **6394**. Jewel or Glove Box, French grey finish, satin lined. length, oval, 11 in.

BARBOUR SILVER CO.
Quadruple Plate.

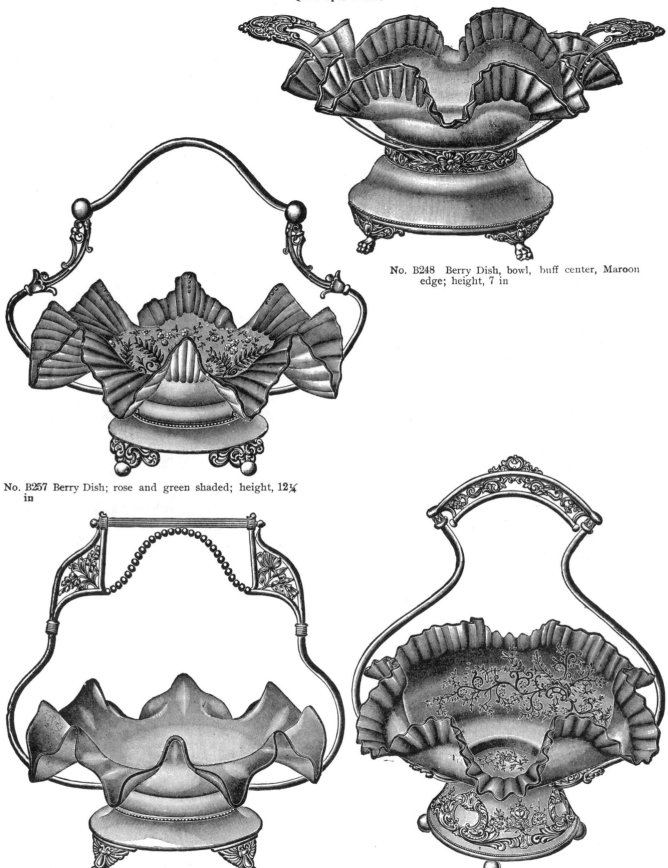

No. B248 Berry Dish, bowl, buff center, Maroon
edge; height, 7 in

No. B257 Berry Dish; rose and green shaded; height, 12¼
in

No. B259 Berry Dish, rose lined; height, 11 in.

No. B253 Berry Dish, rose and buff shaded bowl, gold
decorations; height, 12 in

BARBOUR SILVER CO.

No. B2036 Bowl, gold lined, satin B. C., diameter 9 in.

No. B2225 Cake, satin chased center and border, height 8½ inches

No. B2035 Bowl, gold lined, satin B. C., diameter 9 in.

No. B2037 Bowl, plain burnished, gold lined, diam. 9 in.

No. B117 Cake, bright embossed, diam. 10½ in
Gold lined

No. B116 Cake, satin, burnished embossing diam. 10 in.

No. B2009 Baking Dish
Plain burnished, removable porcelain lining.
Capacity, 3 pints.

No. B2656 Crumb Tray. Satin, B. C.
No. B2656 Crumb Scraper. Satin B. C.
Length Scraper 12 inches.

No. B2006 Baking Dish
Satin, B. C., engraved. Removable Porcelain Lining.
Capacity, 3 pints.

No. B2001 Baking Dish. Satin B. C., Engraved.

No. B2655 Crumb Tray. Satin B. C.
No. B2655 Crumb Scraper. Satin B. C
Length Scraper 8 inches.

No. B2412 Baking Dish.
Removable porcelain lining. Satin B. C. Engraved. Capacity, 3 pints.

GUARANTEED QUADRUPLE PLATE SILVERWARE.

No. W18   Crumb Set, engraved, burnished, ebony handles. Dimensions of tray, 8¾ x5½ in.

No. W20   Crumb Set, repousse, burnished, ebony handle. Dimensions, 5 x 9

No. W9   Crumb Set, satin engraved, bright cut. Dimensions of tray, 7 x 8¾ in.

No. W413   Spoon Tray, burnished; gold lined

No. W60   Gravy Boat and Tray, $8.00, burnished. Length of tray, 9⅜ in; length of boat, 7¼ in

No. W60   Spoon Tray, burnished gold lined. Height, 5¼ in.; length, 8½ in.

GUARANTEED QUADRUPLE PLATE SILVERWARE.

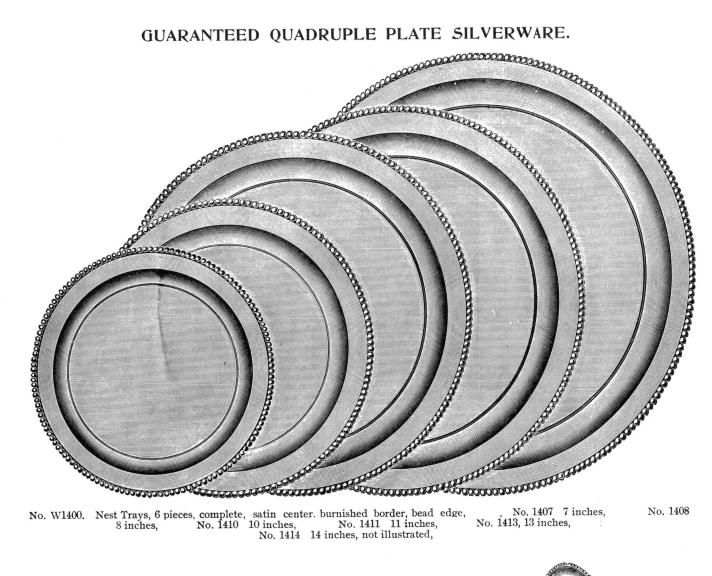

No. W1400. Nest Trays, 6 pieces, complete, satin center. burnished border, bead edge, , No. 1407 7 inches, No. 1408
8 inches, No. 1410 10 inches, No. 1411 11 inches, No. 1413, 13 inches,
No. 1414 14 inches, not illustrated,

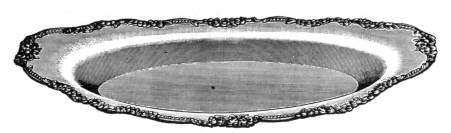

No. W112 Bread Tray, plain burnished, rose border, Dimensions, 13x7¼ in.

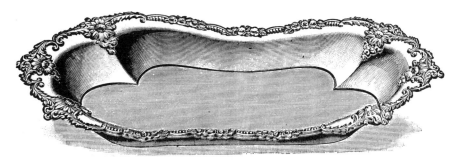

No. W3 Biscuit Tray, burnished (suitable dish for salads, etc.), dimensions.
12½x7¼ inches.

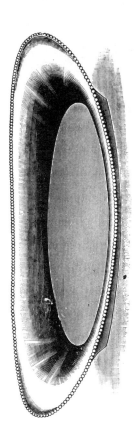

No. W109 Bread Tray, plain burnished, ball bead edge, dimensions 12¼ x6⅞ inches.

Quadruple Silver Plated Trinket, Jewel, Glove and Handkerchief Boxes.

PRICE EACH.

No. 8897. Glove Box. Embossed, Burnished, Satin Lined.

Handkerchief Box. Burnished, Pierced, Satin Lined.
7¾ inches long, 5⅞ inches wide, 4 inches high.
No. 8899.

Handkerchief Box, with Lock. Burnished, Embossed, Satin Lined.
7¾ inches long, 6¼ inches wide, 4½ inches high.
No. 8900.

Square Jewel Box. Embossed, Burnished,
Satin Lined.
No. 8902.

Collar Button Box. Burnished, Pierced.
Illustration one-half size.
No. 8901.

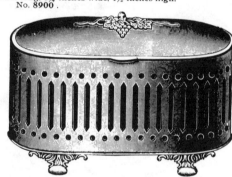

No. 6395. Jewel Box, pierced, burnished,
lined with satin, illustration, one-half
size.

Trinket Box. Burnished and Pierced.
No. 8903.

No. 6392. Jewel Box, satin engraved, ½ size.

Jewel Box. Burnished, Embossed, Satin Lined.
No. 8904.

SILVER PLATED WARE.

MATCH AND TOBACCO BOXES.

Illustrations Full Size.   Prices Each.

No. **6572**.   Smoke Set, with compartment for tobacco, pipe and matches, length 6⅝, width 3½, heigth 2¾ inches, repousse, bright silver, gold lined.

No. **6574**.   Tobacco Box (oval), capacity one-half pound, height 4¼ in., length 5 in., bright silver, gold lined .

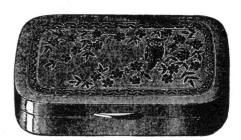

No. **6588**.   Tobacco Box, chased, gold lined, ½ size .

No. **6586**.   Tobacco Box, chased, gold lined.

No. **6587**.   Tobacco Box, satin engraved, gold lined, ½ size.

SILVER PLATED WARE.

CIGAR HOLDER AND ASH RECEIVER (Cut Actual Size)
Sterling Silver, polished; gold lined receiver.
No. T207 Each.

Smoking Set.   Burnished, Gold Lined.   Half size
No. 8851 .

No. **6584**.   Cigar Lamp, burnished.

No. **6546**.   Match Holder
satin engraved, gold lined.
½ size .

No. **6542**.   Match Holder, satin
engraved, gold lined, ½
size

Smoker's Lamp.   Plain Burnished.
No. **8856** .

No. **6543**.   Match Holder, 3
handles, satin engraved,
gold lined, ½ size .

Smoking Set.   Embossed Burnished.
No. 8850 .

No. **6549**.   Match Holder,
satin, gilt lined, ½ scale.

172

Silver Plated
SMOKERS' ARTICLES.
Illustrations About One-Half Size.

No. **6581.** Ash Holder with revolving cover .

No. **6577.** Ash Tray, French gray border, length 8½ inches.

No. **6576.** Banjo Ash Receiver, gold lined, ½ size.

No. **6579.** Combination Ash Tray, Cigar Holder, Cutter and Match Holder .

No. **12.** Cigar cutter, full size . .

No. **6580.** Ash Receiver, satin, ½ scale.

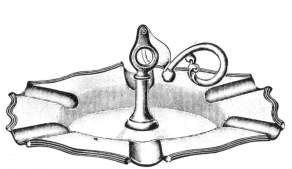

No. **6582.** Ash Tray, Cigar Cutter and Holder.

No. **6583.** Tobacco Jar, gray finish, black inlaid engraving, one-third size.

No. **6578.** Ash Tray and Match Holder, satin engraved, gold lined, illustration two-thirds size .

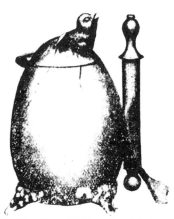

No. **6585.** Cigar Lighter, burnished.

SILVER PLATED WARE.

Safety Match Holder and Cigar Tray.   Plain Burnished.
No. **8860** .

Ash Receiver and Cigar Cutter.   Plain Burnished.
No. **8861** .

Cigar Box.   Capacity, 50 Cigars.   Cedarwood Lining.   Burnished
and Embossed.   No. **8862** .

Tobacco Jar.   Decorated Glass, Silver Plated Cover.
No. **8863** .

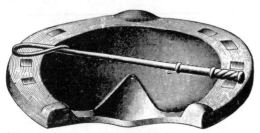

Ash Receiver.   Burnished.   One-half size.
No. **8859** .

Sterling Silver

Pocket Cigar Cutter.   Sterling Silver.
French Grey Finish.   No. **8170** .

Pocket Cigar Cutter.   Sterling Silver.
French Grey Finish.   No. **8171** .

Watch Stand.   Plain Burnished.
No. **8930** .

No. **42.**

Ash Tray.

L'Art Nouveau.

STERLING SILVER

Silver Plated Shaving Sets and Stands

SHAVING SET
Set contains one satin bright cut engraved cup, burnished shield, opal glass soap cup and one fine shaving brush with extra quality bristles. Both pieces are fine quality silver plated. Put up in a sateen lined, leatherette covered presentation case.
No. 1A32041

SHAVING SET
Set contains one burnished finish pierced design cup, opal glass soap cup, and one shaving brush with extra quality bristles. Both pieces are fine quality silver plated. Put up in a sateen lined covered leatherette presentation case.
No. 1A3206

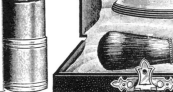

SHAVING SET
Set contains one burnished cup, threaded design, with opal glass soap cup, and one fine shaving brush, with extra quality bristles. Both pieces are high quality silver plated. Put up in a fine strong and durable wood case, leatherette covered, sateen lined.
No. 1A32-40

SHAVING STAND
Combination burnished and French gray finish. 6-inch beveled edge mirror on extension rod. Opal glass soap cup. High grade silver plated; finest quality bristles.
No. 1A32-85

SHAVING STAND
Burnished; 6-inch beveled edge mirror on extension rod. Opal glass soap cup. High grade silver plated; finest quality bristles; tube of soap in container.
No. 1A32-53

SILVER PLATED WARE.
SHAVING SETS.
Illustrations One-half Size.

No. **6439**. Shaving Set, S. B. C., ebony handle, burnished, gold lined.

No. **6436**. Shaving Set, burnished.

No. **6434**. Razor Strop, spring roller.

No. **6440**. Shaving Set, satin engraved, gold lined.

No. **6431**. Shaving Set, S. B. C. G. L., burnished shield, ebony handle, brush.

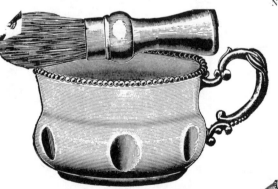

No. **6441**. Shaving Set, burnished, beaded, gold lined, height 2½ in.

No. **6430**. Shaving Set, burnished, gold lined.

No. **6432**. Shaving Cup and Brush, cup fluted and gold lined.

No. **6438**. Shaving Set, satin engraved, gold lined.

SILVER PLATED WARE.

CURLING SETS

TOWEL RING.

Illustrations One-half Size.

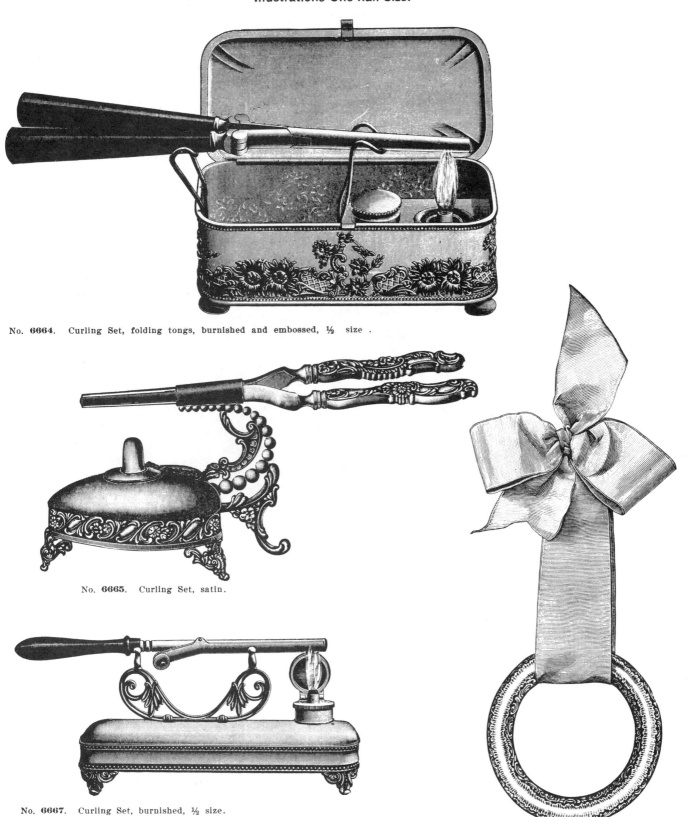

No. **6664**. Curling Set, folding tongs, burnished and embossed, ½ size .

No. **6665**. Curling Set, satin.

No. **6667**. Curling Set, burnished, ½ size.

No. **6666**. Towel Ring, single, with ribbon, ½ size .

BARBOUR SILVER CO.
Quadruple Plate.

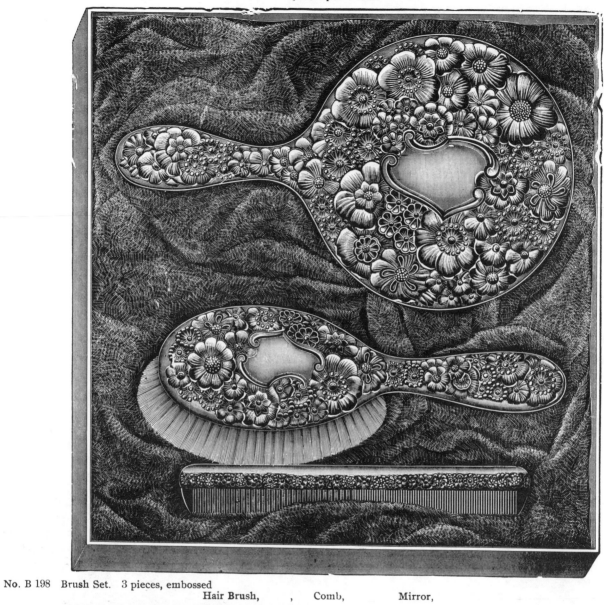

No. B 198   Brush Set.   3 pieces, embossed

Hair Brush,   ,   Comb,   Mirror,

No. B 198   Hat Brush
    Fancy embossed.   Length, 6 inches.

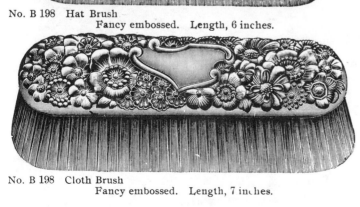

No. B 198   Cloth Brush
    Fancy embossed.   Length, 7 inches.

No. B 20   Puff Box
    Bright embossed.   Height, 3½ inches.

No. B198. Military Brush, fancy embossed, length 4½ inches.

No. B19   Puff Box, satin bright cut, height 2¾ inches.

No. B30   Soap Box, satin, B. C., size 3x4.

No. B29 Soap Box, satin, B. C. center, plain sides, size 3x4 inches.

No. B238 Comb and Brush Tray, satin, burnished sides, size 9½x6½ inches.

No. B198 Whisk Broom, fancy embossed, length 10½ inches.

No. B29 Soap Box, plain, burnished, ball bead, size, 3x4 inches

No. B239 Comb and Brush Tray, satin, rococco edge, size 9½x6½ inches.

SILVER PLATED WARE.

SOAP BOXES, GAME COUNTERS.

Illustrations One-Half Size.

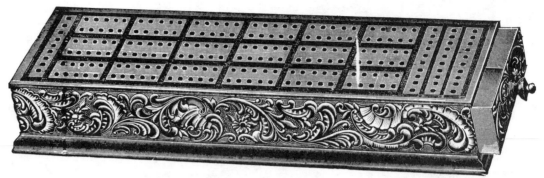

No. **6639.** Cribbage Board .

No. **6640.** Game Counter .

No. **6641.** Game Counter .

No. **6642.** Playing Card Case, with cards.

No. **6643.** Poker Set, with cards and chips.

No. **6650.** Soap Box, satin, gold lined.

No **6645.** Soap Dish, satin, gold lined.

No. **6646.** Soap Box, burnished, applied Dec., gold lined

No. **6647.** Soap Box, embossed, one-half size .

SILVER PLATED WARE.
Call Bells

Call Bell. Rotary Strike,
Silver Plated.
No. 8879.

Call Bell. Rotary Strike, Silver Plated.
No. 8880.

Call Bell. Rotary Strike, Silver Plated.
No. 8878.

Illustrations About One-half Size.

Tap Bell. Bronze Base.
No. 8874.

Hand Bell. Oxidized Silver.
No. 8875.

Hand Bell. Silver Plated.
No. 8876.

Tap Bell. Bronze Base.
No. 8877.

No. 6759. Silver plated Bell,
polished gold base.

No. 6760. Silver Plated Bell,
polished gold relief base.

No. 6761. Electric, all silver
plated, patented.

No. 6762. Bell, silver plated.

No. 6765. Electric Stroke
Bell.

181

SILVER PLATED WARE.

INK STANDS.

Illustrations One-Half Size.

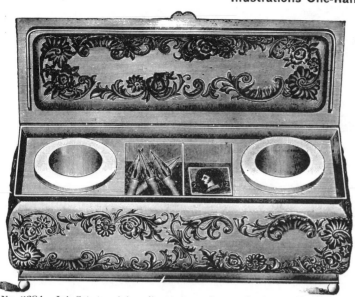

No. **6684**. Ink Set, two ink wells, stamp and pen point boxes, dimensions 6x2¼ inches, height 2 inches.

No. **6695**. Mucilage Pot, glass lined, with tray

No. **6689**. Ink Set, burnished, beaded. 2½ inch bottle.

No. **6694**. Ink, bright silver, cut glass, ½ scale .

No. **6692**. Roll Blotter, silver, dimensions 4x2⅞ in.

No. **6688**. Ink Stand, satin, cut glass.

No. **6686**. Writing Set, cut glass bottles, length 6½ in.

Price Guide

The prices in this book have been arrived at by averaging out the items offered for sale throughout various tradepapers, auction s, flea markets, antique shows and private dealers. These prices are only a guide as they may from one region to another. **Remember, this is only a guide. We are not in the business of buying or selling merchandise in this book.**

Page 15
All on this page are $55-65

Page 16
All on this page are $40-60

Page 17
All on this page are $60-80

Page 18
No. C1920- $60-70
No. C192 - $50-60
No. C1321 - $120-140
No. C1676 - $80-100
No. C207 - $60-70
No. C1678 - $75-80
No. C173 - $100-130
No. C204 - $60-70
No. C509 - $100-120
No. C11 - $60-70
No. C213 - $70-80
No. C1464 - $80-90
No. C1735 - 100-120

Page 19
All on this page are $15-25

Page 20
No. 7046 - $110-130
No. 5350 - $70-90
No. 5333 - $60-80
No. 5337 - $50-60
No. 5484 - $50-60

Page 21
No. 7039 - $110-130
No. 5345 - $110-130
No. 5341 - $70-80
No. 5349 - $80-110

Page 22
No. 5347 - $110-130
No. 7056 - $70-80
No. 7052 - $55-65

Page 23
No. 7040 - $130-140
No. 7057 - $70-80
No. 5335 - $70-80
No. 5335 - $75-100

Page 24
No. 7036 - $80-110
No. 5485 - $60-70
No. 5486 - $60-70
No. 7034 - $80-110

Page 25
No. B10 - $40-60
No. B11 - $30-40
No. B12 - $10-20

Page 26
No. B73 - $50-60
No. B74 - $30-40
No. B75 - $10-20

Page 27
No. B52 - $40-60
No. B53 - $30-40
No. B54 - $10-20

Page 28
All on this page are $30-40

Page 29
No. 5320 - $150+
No. 5323 - $60-70
No. 5321 - $60-70
No. 5319 - $80-100
No. 5324 - $80-100

Page 30
All on this page are $70-80

Page 31
No. 6433 - $80-100
No. 5489 - $40-50
No. 8001 - $40-50

No. 5488 - $40-50
No. 8000 - $40-50
No. 5490 - $40-50
No. 5487 - $40-50
No. 6437 - $30-40
No. 6435 - $100-120

Page 32
All on this page are $50-60

Page 33
No. 8056 - $40-50
No. 8057 - $50-60
No. 8058 - $30-40
No. 8059 - $25-35
No. 5430 - $40-50
No. 5429 - $20-30
No. 5431 - $30-40
No. 5433 - $100-120

Page 34
No. 5451 - $100-120
No. 5452 - $30-40
No. 5453 - $30-40
No. 5457 - $30-40
No. 5454 - $30-40
No. 5456 - $60-80
No. 5462 - $40-50
No. 5460 - $30-40
No. 5461 - $30-40

Page 35
All on this page are $50-55
Except
No. 1242 - $60-70
No. 1247 - $300+

Page 36
No. 8156 - $225-250
No. 8157 - $175-200
No. 8158 - $175-200
No. 8159 - $200-225
No. 8160 - $130-150
No. 8161 - $120-130

No. 8162 - $120-140
No. 8163 - $130-140
No. 8164 - $120-140
No. 8165 - $130-150
No. 8166 - $120-130
No. 8167 - $130-150

Page 37
All on this page are $125-150
Except:
No. 5860 - $200+
No. 5859 - $250+
No. 5868 - $80-100
No. 5861 - $175-200

Page 38
All on this page are $80-100

Page 39
All on this page are $80-100

Page 40
All on this page are $75-100
Except:
No. 5886 - $110-125
No. 8096 - $40-60
No. 8094 - $40-60

Page 41
All on this page are $150-175

Page 42
No. 8881 - $150+
No. 6610 - $150+
No. 8882 - $200+
No. 6609 - $175+
No. 6608 - $200+

Page 43
No. 8111 - $40-50
No. 8112 - $40-50

No. 8118 - $30-40
No. 8113 - $60-70
No. 8119 - $30-40
No. 8114 - $30-40
No. 8115 - $40-50
No. 8116 - $40-50
No. 8122 - $30-40
No. 8121 - $30-40
No. 8124 - $30-40

Page 44
All on this page are
$75-100

Page 45
All on this page are
$100-125
Except:
No. 1A2-55 - $100-150

Page 46
All on this page are
$100-125

Page 47
No. 6494 - $300-400
No. 6510 - $200-300
No. 6501 - $175-225
No. 6498 - $200-300
No. 6497 - $200-300
No. 6502 - $200-300

Page 48
All on this page are
$200-400

Page 49
No. B3470 - $40-50
No. B3471 - $40-50
No. B3472 - $50-60
No. B3463 - $40-50
No. B3464 - $30-40
No. B3465 - $30-40
No. B3475 - $60-80
No. B3476 - $100-120
No. B3477 - $120-140
No. B3468 - $30-40
No. B3469 - $30-40
No. B3478 - $110-130
No. B3473 - $70-90
No. B3474 - $100-120

Page 50
No. B3392 - $50-60
No. B3393 - $30-40
No. B3396 - $60-70
No. B3397 - $30-40
No. B3405 - $100-150
No. B3414 - $60-80

No. B3433 - $60-80
No. B3434 - $70-90
No. B3404 - $50-60
No. B3413 - $50-70

Page 51
No. B3436 - $80-100
No. B3423 - $60-80
No. B3424 - $80-110
No. B3394 - $50-60
No. B3395 - $30-40
No. B3437 - $125-175
No. B3438 - $125-175

Page 52
All on this page are
$75-100

Page 53
All on this page are
$60-80

Page 54
All on this page are
$40-60

Page 55
No. 5764 - $40-50
No. 5762 - $40-50
No. 5763 - $80-100
No. 5767 - $50-60
No. 5766 - $50-60

Page 56
All on this page are
$75-100

Page 57
All on this page are
$30-50

Page 58
All on this page are
$75-90

Page 59
All on this page are
$80-100

Page 60
VASES
8 inch - $50-75
10 inch - $75-100
12 inch - $75-100
14 inch - $100-125

CANDLESTICKS
8 inch - $50-70
10 inch - $60-80
12 inch - $60-80
14 inch - $110-140

Page 61
No. C1452 - $75-100
No. C1019 - $75-100
No. C1016 - $75-100
No. C1104 - $75-100
No. C1014 - $75-100
No. C1109 - $75-100
No. C1115 - $75-100
No. C73 - $75-100
No. C215 - $125-175
No. C71 - $75-100

Page 62
No. C20 - $75-100
No. C180 - $70-90
No. C181 - $70-90
No. C301 - $30-40
No. C435 - $40-60
No. C511 - $70-90
No. C27 - $40-50
No. C1921 - $75-100
No. C301 - $40-50
No. C1641 - $75-100
No. C225 - $40-50
No. C227 - $50-75
No. C228 - $70-90
No. C1791 - $80-100

Page 63
No. 6448 - $125-150
No. 6449 - $125-150
No. 6450 - $75-100
No. 6451 - $75-100
No. 6452 - $75-100
No. 6453 - $80-90
No. 6454 - $80-90

Page 64
No. C1553-SB - $75-100
No. C1553-CP - $75-100
No. C1553-CP - $125-160
No. C1553-TP - $125-160
No. C1555-TP - $80-100
No. C1555-SB - $70-90
No. C1555-CP - $70-90
No. C1980 - $70-90
No. C1452 - $90-110

Page 65
Butter Knife - $60-80
Cold Meat Fork - $60-80
Sugar Spoon - $60-80
Fish Fork - $60-80
Coffee Spoon - $40-60
Fish Knife - $100-130

Page 66
Ice Cream Server - $100-130
Soup Ladle - $125-150
Gravy Ladle - $80-100
Cream Ladle - $70-90
Ice Cream Spoon - $70-90
Sugar Tongs - $60-80

Page 67
Small Berry Spoon - $80-100
Pickle Fork - $60-80
Salad Fork - $80-100
Oyster Fork - $75-90
Large Berry Spoon - $100-140

Page 68
Small Berry Spoon - $80-100
Pickle Fork - $60-80
Salad Fork - $80-100
Oyster Fork - $75-90
Nut Spoon - $60-80

Page 69
Olive Fork - $50-70
Bon Bon Spoon - $40-50
Sugar Spoon - $50-60
Coffee Spoon - $30-40
Large Berry Spoon - $80-100
Sugar Tongs - $60-80

Page 70
Sugar Sifter - $80-100
Cold Meat Fork - $80-100
Cream Ladle - $80-100
Gravy Ladle - $80-100
Soup Ladle - $110-130
Olive Spoon - $30-40

Page 71
All on this page are
$50-75
Except:
No. 700 Cream L - $60-80
Provence Cream L - $70-90
Orange Spoon - $60-80

Page 72
Butter Knives - $50-75
Sugar Spoon - $75-100

Page 73
Sugar - $75-100
Cream - $75-100
Cold Meat - $75-100
Tomato Server - $100-120
Sugar - $60-80
Jelly - $60-80
Olive - $60-80
Sardine - $60-80
Berry - $60-80

Page 74
All on this page are
$75-100

Page 75
All on this page are
$125-150

Page 76
Mustard Spoon - $30-50
Others - $125-150

Page 77
Fish Set - $125+
Salad Set - $125+
Berry - $100-125
Cream Ladle - $60-80
Ice Cream Spoon - $50-75
Orange Spoon - $50-75
Oyster Fork - $40-60

Page 78
Venus Set - $75-100
Oyster Forks - $100-150
Bread Fork - $70-90
Sugar - $30-50
Butter - $30-50

Page 79
All on this page are
$50-70

Page 80
Cream Ladle - $50-75
Berry Set - $150-175
Sugar Sifter - $50-75
Ice Tongs - $40-50
Sugar Shell - $40-60
Sardine Fork - $50-60
Coffee Spoon Set - $100-120

Page 81
All on this page are
$10-20

Page 82
No. 647 - $40-60
No. 681 - $10-20
No. 703 - $30-50
No. 604 - $20-40
No. 615 - $40-60
No. 657 - $60-80
No. 638 - $40-60

Page 83
No. 702 - $60-80
No. 701 - $40-60
No. 708 - $70-90
No. 709 - $70-90
No. 706 - $60-80
No. 638 - $30-50
No. 710 - $30-50

Page 84
PLATED
All on this page are
$10-20

Page 85
PLATED
All on this page are
$10-20

Page 86
PLATED
All on this page are
$10-20

Page 87
PLATED
All on this page are
$15-25

Page 88
PLATED
No. 154 - $20-40
No. 155 - $20-40
Pie Server - $10-20
Sugar & Butter - $10-20

Page 89
PLATED
All on this page are
$15-20

Page 90
PLATED
Set - $20-30
Others - $10-20

Page 91
Cheese Scoop - $10-20
Sets All - $20-40

Page 92
Sets - $20-30
Knives - $10-20

Page 93
All on this page are
$20-30

Page 94
All on this page are
$10-20

Page 95
All on this page are
$10-20

Page 96
Fork - $10-20
Sets - $10-30

Page 97
All on this page are
$10-20

Page 98
All on this page are
$15-25

Page 99
Sets - $20-30
Others - $15-20

Page 100
Berry Spoon - $15-30
Others - $10-20

Page 101
All on this page are
$10-20

Page 102
Sets - $15-30
Cold Meat Fork - $20-30

Page 103
Sets - $15-30
Jelly - $10-20

Page 104
Coffee Spoon - $10-15
Others - $10-20

Page 105
All on this page are
$10-20

Page 106
All on this page are
$15-25

Page 107
All on this page are
$10-25

Page 108
Sets - $15-30
Others - $10-20

Page 109
Both - $125-150

Page 110
Each - $50-60

Page 111
No. D1069 - $30-40
No. D3445 - $20-30
No. D4824 - $40-50
No. D3445 Tray - $30-40
No. D4817 - $50-60
Walters - $30-60

Page 112
All on this page are
$20-40

Page 113
All on this page are
$20-40

Page 114
No. B2312 - $30-40
No. B20 - $30-40
No. B2309 - $30-40
No. B16 - $40-50
No. B2313 - $30-40
No. B13-15 - $40-50
No. B2180 - $50-70
No. B2169 - $40-50

Page 115
No. B2001 - $50-70
No. B9 - $40-50

No. B11 - $30-40
No. B2078 - $30-40
No. B10 - $30-40
No. B236 - $30-40
No. B235 - $30-40
No. B12 - $30-40

Page 116
All on this page are
$30-40
Except:
No. B2079 - $40-50
No. B2080 - $5$30-40-$30-40
No. B11 - $40-50

Page 117
No. B18 - $100-120
No. B2421 - $60-70
No. B2420 - $60-75

Page 118
No. B31 - $40-50
No. B64 - $50-60
No. B778 - $60-80
No. B60 - $50-60
No. B2421 - $40-50
No. B2422 - $40-50
No. B62 - $50-60
No. B2423 - $40-50
No. B29 - $40-50

Page 119
Both - $125-150

Page 120
Both - $125-150

Page 121
Both - $125-150

Page 122
No. W19 - $60-80
No. W62 - $60-80
No. W69 - $120-130
No. W220 - $50-70

Page 123
All on this page are
$75-100

Page 124
All on this page are
$60-80

Page 125
All on this page are
$60-80

Page 126
All on this page are
$60-80

Page 127
All on this page are
$70-90

Page 128
All on this page are
$90-110

Page 129
All on this page are
$100-120

Page 130
All on this page are
$40-50

Page 131
No. 6327 - $100-150
No. 6329 - $50-60
No. 8813 - $50-60
No. 6331 - $80-100

Page 132
No. 6325 - $40-50
No. 6337 - $40-50
No. 8813 - $50-60
No. 6331 - $80-100

Page 133
No. W060 Syrup - $40-50
No. W60 Tray - $30-40
No. W60 Butter - $40-60
No. W60 Set - $175-200

Page 134
No. B2170 - $60-70
No. B2169 - $30-40
No. B2163½ - $30-40
No. B2162 - $70-80

Page 135
No. A0293 Set - $175-200
Butter - $50-60
Urn - $80-100
Syrup - $50-60

Page 136
All on this page are
$60-80

Page 137
All on this page are
$80-100+

Page 138
All on this page are
$20-40

Page 139
No. A815 - $100-120
No. A55 - $40-50
No. A56 - $30-40
No. A30 - $30-40
No. A1 - $30-40
No. A69 - $60-80
No. A67 - $70-90
No. A813 - $50-60
No. A56 - $50-70

Page 140
All on this page are
$60-80

Page 141
All on this page are
$80-100+

Page 142
All on this page are
$60-80

Page 143
No. M0107 - $40-50
No. M0108 - $40-50
Waiters - $30-50
No. M0109 - $40-50
No. M110 - $60-70
No. M111 - $60-70

Page 144
No. W31 - $70-80
No. W0401 - $60-70
No. W20 - $80-100
No. W399 - $60-80
No. W59 - $30-40
No. W331 - $30-40

Page 145
All on this page are
$40-60
Except:
No. W662 - $50-70
No. W87 - $150-200

Page 146
No. A811 - $100+
No. A812 - $125-150
No. A96 - $125-150
No. A408 - $125+
No. A11 - $125+

Page 147
Cups - $30-40
Salts - $30-40

Page 148
No. W191 - $150-200
No. W189 - $200+
No. W182 - $100+
No. W163 - $150+

Page 149
No. 8809 - $50-60
No. 8810 - $70-80
No. 8811 - $100-120
No. 8812 - $50-60

Page 150
No. 6139 - $150-200
No. 6140 - $150-200
No. 6164 - $75-100
No. 8840 - $75-100
No. 8841 - $75-100
No. 6141 - $150-200

Page 151
No. 6136 - $150-200
No. 6137 - $80-100
No. 6138 - $150-200
No. 6167 - $80-100
No. 6165 - $80-100
No. 6166 - $80-100

Page 152
All on this page are
$175+

Page 153
All on this page are
$40-50
Except:
No. 6476 - $50-60

Page 154
No. 6467 - $40-60
No. 6468 - $40-50
No. 6469 - $40-50
No. 8787 - $50-60
No. 8802 - $30-40
No. 8794 - $40-60
No. 8789 - $50-60
No. 8790 - $60-70
No. 8792 - $50-60
No. 8791 - $60-70
No. 8788 - $30-40
No. 8796 - $40-60

Page 155
No. 6249 - $70-80
No. 6236 - $40-60
No. 6237 - $50-60
No. 6228 - $40-50
No. 6229 - $60-70
No. 6245 - $60-80

Page 156
No. 6349 - $250+
No. 6360 - $80-100
No. 6356 - $30-50
No. 6358 - $30-50
No. 6359 - $30-40
No. 6361 - $60-70
No. 6355 - $30-40

Page 157
All on this page are
$40-50

Page 158
No. 6551 - $30-40
No. 6553 - $30-40
No. 6552 - $40-60
No. 6545 - $30-40
No. 6544 - $30-40
No. 8857 - $50-75
No. 6541 - $70-80
No. 6555 - $30-40
No. 6548 - $50-60
No. 6554 - $30-40
No. 6547 - $30-40
No. 6539 - $70-90
No. 6550 - $30-40
No. 8858 - $30-40

Page 159
No. B27 - $30-40
No. B103 - $30-40
No. B114 - $30-40
No. B135 - $30-40
No. B137 - $30-40
No. B139 - $30-40
No. B7 - $100-150
No. B131 - $30-40
No. B8 - $100-150
No. B22 - $100-150
No. B67 - $100-150

Page 160
All on this page are
$30-40

Page 161
All on this page are
$75-100

Page 162
All on this page are
$100+

Page 163
No. 2064 - $80-100
No. 2065 - $80-100
No. 8855 - $50-75
No. 6723 - $60-80
No. B3510 - $30-40
No. 6714 - $60-80
No. 8852 - $50-75
No. 2066 - $100-120

Page 164
All on this page are
$50-70

Page 165
All on this page are
$100-150

Page 166
All on this page are
$60-80

Page 167
No. B2656 - $30-40
No. B2655 - $30-40
All others - $75-100

Page 168
All on this page are
$40-60

Page 169
All on this page are
$30-50

Page 170
All on this page are
$40-60
Except:
No. 8897 - $80-100
No. 8900 - $80-100

Page 171
No. 6572 - $100-150
No. 6574 - $150-200
No. 6586 - $75-100
No. 6588 - $40-50
No. 6587 - $40-50

Page 172
All on this page are
$60-80
Except:
No. 6584 - $150-200
No. 8850 - $100-150
No. 8856 - $100-150

Page 173
All on this page are
$100-150
Except:
No. 6579 - $150-200
No. 6583 - $150-200
No. 6578 - $100-150
No. 6585 - $150-200

Page 174
All on this page are
$40-50
Except: No. 42 - $100-150
No. 8860 - $75-100
No. 8861 - $100-150
No. 8862 - $80-100
No. 8863 - $125-175
No. 8859 - $50-75
No. 8930 - $40-60
No. 8170 - $75-100
No. 8171 - $60-80

Page 175
No. 1A32041 - $60-80
No. 1A3206 - $60-80
No. 1A32-85 - $75-100
No. 1A32-53 - $75-100
No. 1A32-40 - $50-75

Page 176
All on this page are
$60-80

Page 177
No. 6664 - $80-100
No. 6665 - $60-80
No. 6667 - $60-80
No. 6666 - $15-30

Page 178
No. B198 Set - $50-60
No. B198HB - $10-20
No. B198CB - $10-20
No. B20 - $30-40

Page 179
All on this page are
$30-40

Page 180
All on this page are
$60-80
Except:
No. 6639 - $100-150

Page 181
All on this page are
$40-60

Page 182
No. 6684 - $100-150
No. 6695 - $60-80
No. 6694 - $100-150
No. 6689 - $100-150
No. 6692 - $30-40
No. 6688 - $100-150
No. 6686 - $125-175

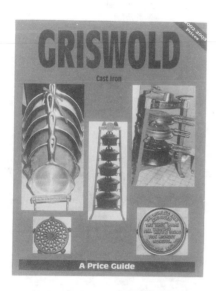
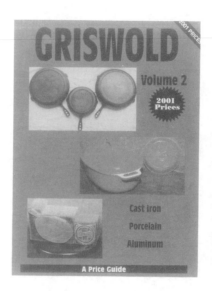

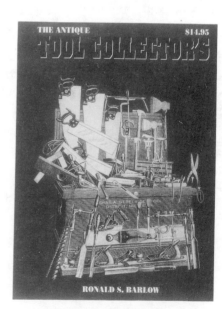